Family Time Reading Fun

Helping Your Child Become a Successful Reader

Written by Linda McCorkel Clinard, Ph.D.
University of California, Irvine

Editor: Joellyn Thrall Cicciarelli

Illustrator: Jill Dubin

Project Director: Carolea Williams

CTP © 1997 Creative Teaching Press, Inc., Cypress, CA 90630

Table of Contents

Introduction

● ●

Have you ever wanted to help your child become a better reader, writer, and all-around student, but didn't know how? *Family Time Reading Fun: Helping Your Child Become a Successful Reader* provides **ideas** for a myriad of fun ways to help your child become a better thinker, listener, speaker, reader, and writer; **information** to explain why each activity is important; and ready-to-reproduce **resources**. Keep the following principles in mind as you use *Family Time Reading Fun:*

● Literacy is more than just reading and writing. Literacy is the ability to use thinking, speaking, listening, reading, and writing to solve problems; complete tasks; and communicate wants, needs, feelings, and ideas.

● A literate child is a successful child.

● Literacy is part of our everyday lives—at home, work and play; in stores, the car, and restaurants; and in every school subject.

● Parents do the right thing! You should pat yourself on the back for the many "right things" you do to improve your child's literacy.

● Parent participation in literacy activities has a direct and significant effect on children's literacy growth.

● The activities apply to children of various experience levels—both struggling and good listeners, speakers, and readers; children for whom English is a second language; and gifted children.

● The information is for all families—two-parent and single-parent families; grandparent-led families; families in inner cities, suburbs, and rural communities; and families of all income levels and cultural backgrounds.

Family Time Reading Fun offers a well-rounded approach to assist you in helping your child become a better reader and all-around student. The information provided in this resource helps answer these all-important questions—*What is literacy? Why is literacy important? How can I tell if my child needs help? How can I help my child become literate and succeed in school?* and *What will my child gain from literacy activities?* Here's a preview of the valuable information you'll find.

You will become familiar with literacy background and concepts when you read the Ten Keys to Literacy. After reading, keep this information in mind when guiding your child through the activities.

Explanations of five major influences on your child's reading, writing, and overall academic success are included in the section called Influences on Literacy Development. When it's time for some "family time reading fun," consult the questions at the beginning of each activity section before choosing activities. After reading the questions, choose from the dozens of everyday literacy activities that make learning fun. The purpose of each activity is explained, and an easy-to-read materials list helps with activity setup. Activities are designed primarily for kindergarten through third grade—and can be adapted to other levels, as needed. Once you choose activities, you're ready... ready to get involved, ready to help your child learn, and ready to have fun!

Ten Keys to Literacy

• •

The following are ten important concepts for you to keep in mind as you guide your child to literacy. These "ten keys to literacy" are part of every-day experiences, and their importance is confirmed in professional literature and teaching practices. Read the information in this section to learn more about the "ten keys to literacy" and their importance to your child.

1 **Literacy is more than knowing how to read and write.** When we are literate, we use thinking, speaking, listening, reading, and writing to solve problems; complete tasks; and communicate wants, needs, feelings, and ideas. Literacy applies to many areas of life. We can be literate in everyday spoken languages from a variety of cultures; in professional or technical languages such as a computer language; in a code language, such as Morse Code; in mathematical languages; and in subject-specific terminology, such as medical terms or terms relating to sports and hobbies.

2 **Everyone has literacy strengths.** We all differ in how and why we think, listen, speak, read, and write, but each of us has strengths in one or more of these areas. (For example, Bill may write more clearly than Jim, but Jim may speak more confidently than Bill.) We tend to try harder when we are aware of what we do well. Whether you are the learner or the teacher, you should *stress strengths and nurture needs.* In other words, you should show pride in and build on your child's literacy accomplishments as you lovingly and respectful-ly nurture his or her needs.

3 **Literacy requires us to become involved and use words for many purposes and in many ways. Involvement helps us become literate.** When your child interacts with others in meaningful everyday experiences, he or she is involved. When your child uses his or her senses (hearing, seeing, tasting, touching, smelling) to gather information, he or she is involved. When your child works diligently to reach goals, he or she is involved. When your child applies literacy in all areas of study—mathematics, social science, physical science, the arts—he or she is involved. When your child is grown and applies literacy in the workplace, in technology, medicine, or business, he or she is involved.

4 **Literacy is a process, not a product.** The literacy process begins at infancy and grows through a lifetime. Preparation for literacy begins when your child, as an infant, sees, hears, smells, tastes, and touches the world around him or her. As your infant, toddler, or young child creates meaning from his or her sensory perceptions, the groundwork for literacy is being laid. Educational and life experiences build on real-world knowledge, and the literacy process continues. For each of us, the literacy process continues throughout our lives.

5 **Progress in literacy cannot be measured by test scores and grades alone.** Checklists, report cards, and test scores can be helpful indicators of where your child is in the literacy process, but they should not be accepted as the final word. Literacy should be measured by observing, recording, and keeping samples of how thinking, listening, speaking, reading, and writing are meaningfully applied in a child's daily life. (For more information on test scores, see pages 18 to 20.)

7 **Specific goals are needed to help children succeed.** Parents often feel they are battling between what they know children need to develop literacy and what public pressure says they need. To resist pressure from others, parents need to focus on four goals to help children succeed in literacy and life.

- *Help children feel safe to try.* We learn best when we feel safe to take risks, and can try out new ideas and learn from past mistakes. To help your child feel safe, praise accomplishments (even the small ones) and focus on what he or she does well.

- *Help children take responsibility for their own learning.* When we create a safe environment (such as a quiet place to study), provide opportunities to explore (such as neighborhood nature walks), and ask questions that prompt thinking (such as *Why do you think the recipe did not work?*), we help children develop responsibility for their learning.

- *Help children be everyday learners.* Children learn from everyday experiences. We need to encourage and guide children to use literacy in everyday life. Everyday experiences include reading together, gardening together, and participating in the activities described on pages 21 to 107.

- *Help children develop a purpose for learning.* We need to guide children to see the importance of activities that involve thinking, speaking, listening, reading, and writing. One easy way to demonstrate a purpose for these activities is to simply explain how a literacy activity in which your child is currently engaged will help in the future (with a job, the family, or everyday tasks).

6 **Children develop literacy skills at different rates and in different ways.** No two children are created the same, and no two learn in the same way. Some children best obtain information through the sense of hearing, some through sight, and others through becoming physically engaged. Your child has natural strengths/talents in areas such as math, music, sports, or language.

8 Factors such as background, resources, and expectations influence literacy development. Ask yourself *How do the following factors impact my child's literacy development?*

● Background—age, grade, interests, attitude, physical characteristics, health, educational and assessment experiences.

● Choice and availability of resources—books, computer programs, games, teachers, tutors, specialists, toys, menus, television.

● Expectations—at home; at school; at a church, temple, or mosque.

These factors influence how children grow in their literacy development. (For an in-depth explanation of how attitude, health, expectations, and educational experiences and resources influence literacy development, see pages 9 to 20.)

9 Literacy is not instant. In our world of "instant" everything, we need to make a conscious effort to be patient. Since literacy skills develop in various ways and at various times for each individual, we should wait and guide our child according to his or her own timetable.

10 Helping with literacy development requires us to be practical and to avoid applying pressure. We should offer practical literacy experiences that fit meaningfully into our children's daily lives. Practical literacy experiences can include reading to and with our children, writing to and with our children, and completing the activities on pages 21 to 107.

We should avoid applying pressure and offer guidance. Pressure works "behind" children and pushes them along; children are not fully aware of the goal they are trying to achieve. On the other hand, children who are guided assume ownership and take responsibility. The following are excellent ways to offer guidance instead of applying pressure: Invite children to choose activities in which to participate. Praise children for accomplishments, even small ones. Ask questions about experiences and listen to children's responses. Help children self-evaluate and set their own goals.

We should be guides, examples, and supporters as we work to apply the "ten keys to literacy" at school, at home, and in the real world.

Influences on Literacy Development

Even before children enter school, parents are filled with questions. *Why is Jason succeeding while Jeremy is not? They have both been given the same opportunities.* Parents try to offer similar opportunities and support, but there is more to consider.

You, your child, and his or her teacher can offer insight into five significant areas that influence literacy learning, regardless of your child's age or background. Exploring these influences can help you understand why children from the same home with similar experiences differ in their literacy success. When considering areas of influence, keep in mind how each can act upon another to either compound a literacy problem or enhance development.

Attitude

How does your child respond when faced with opportunities to speak, listen, read, and write in daily life?

Physical Characteristics

Are vision, hearing, eating habits, sleeping habits, or other physical factors helping or hindering your child's literacy growth?

Expectations

How do adults' expectations and actions influence your child's literacy development?

Educational Experiences and Resources

Is your child exposed to a variety of educational resources and positive experiences that enhance literacy development?

Assessment Experiences

Are you and the teacher using assessment information in the most effective way to encourage your child's literacy progress and plan his or her curriculum?

Attitude

A child's level of interest and attitude greatly influence literacy learning. Each child is motivated to learn depending upon his or her interest in certain subjects, ideas, and assignments. If asked to read about dinosaurs, some first graders may become disinterested and ask, *What does this say? Can't you just read it for me?*, while others become excited and eagerly tackle new words. Consider the following literacy skills and how attitudes and interest levels can influence them.

Thinking

As your child develops an interest in a school- or home-related subject, he or she will begin to think about, formulate opinions about, and care about it. When your child thinks and cares about his or her learning, he or she will take risks and responsibility for the learning.

Listening

Encourage your child to listen, and at the same time challenge him or her to talk about what he or she has heard. When your child does not seem interested in potentially interesting subjects and experiences, do not remain silent. Talk about it, and encourage your child to participate so he or she has the opportunity to develop an interest.

Speaking

Your child naturally talks about what interests him or her. Continue those discussions and enhance them by asking open-ended questions. As your child speaks more and more frequently, he or she will become confident and gain a positive attitude about speaking.

Reading

Attitude and interest make a difference in how much your child chooses to read independently. Be sure to surround your child with reading material that interests him or her, even if it is not reading material you find interesting. Be an example. Let your child see you read every day—whether you read a map, recipe, newspaper, or television guide.

Writing

Because writing is a process, and generally takes longer to complete than other literacy tasks (such as reading and speaking), a child may need extra motivation to sustain interest. Be sure to have your child write about subjects that interest him or her.

As parents, we must constantly be aware of what motivates *each* child as we try to develop literacy activities and incentives to enhance learning. Pages 99 to 108 offer questions and activities to help your child improve his or her attitude and gain a greater interest in literacy-related tasks.

Physical Characteristics

There are a number of physical characteristics that can influence your child's literacy development. Vision and hearing are closely related to literacy performance. Eating and sleeping habits and other health-related issues can influence your child's literacy learning as well.

Vision

Visual frustration can greatly influence your child's reading, writing, speaking, and listening success. If your child uses all of his or her concentration trying to focus on a visual object, he or she is less likely to read or write well, hear directions clearly, or give thoughtful verbal responses.

As parents, we might think a child is being stubborn if he or she refuses to complete an assignment or answer a question that requires visual observation. Such signs of discomfort may be signs of a vision problem. If you suspect your child's eyes are contributing to frustrations in learning to read and write, be sure your child has a thorough visual examination. (See page 108 for a list of questions to help determine if your child needs a vision examination.) Be certain to describe to the optometrist or other vision specialist the behaviors you observe as your child reads and writes. A description of behaviors provides important clues for prescribing solutions.

Glasses do not ensure success in or smooth sailing toward literacy. Your child may need a change in behavior or a little extra help from you or the teacher. However, changes in eyeglass-wearing habits may be all it takes to send your child on the road to literacy. When glasses are recommended, parents and teachers often hear *I can't find my glasses*. Many parents discover that even when the glasses go to school, teachers rarely see them. A primary goal for parents and teachers should be to help children discover the positive impact visual support has on learning.

Hearing

The ability to hear has a great influence on literacy success. Children who have frequent ear problems (fluid buildup, infections, severe allergies) can become frustrated with literacy-related tasks. Phonemic awareness (identifying and manipulating sounds that are heard) can be difficult. Listening to a story or understanding word meanings can also be a challenge.

Be aware of everyday signals that your child's ability to hear is hindering literacy growth. Signals could include standing extremely close to you when you are speaking, not answering questions or refusing to answer questions, or talking more loudly than others. If you suspect your child may have a hearing problem, note the behaviors and ask to have his or her hearing tested.

Timing is very important when hearing is tested. Screenings at school or the doctor's office might occur when an allergy or infection is not present. If you suspect allergies may affect hearing, ask that your child's hearing be tested at a later date. Talk with the teacher if you believe your child's ability to hear is affecting how he or she learns. Your pediatrician, school nurse, or school speech and language pathologist should observe and test hearing at various times throughout the year.

Eating and Sleeping Habits

Eating and sleeping habits influence literacy success in a variety of ways. Good eating and sleeping habits give your child the energy to remain alert in class throughout the day. If your child gets proper nutrition and enough sleep, he or she will have a strong immune system, resulting in better attention at school as well as a superior attendance record.

Poor eating and sleeping habits can adversely influence literacy development. For example, some children seem to have a sensitivity to caffeine or sugar, causing a lack of concentration in school or trouble falling asleep at night. Others seem to become "silly" or physically active. If you feel your child may be affected by caffeine or sugar, modify his or her diet and watch for a change in behavior.

Avoiding breakfast is another eating habit that can adversely affect school performance. Children who skip breakfast often lack the energy to be attentive until lunchtime. Encourage your child to eat a healthy breakfast even if it is nontraditional, such as a sandwich or cottage cheese.

If you suspect your child is negatively influenced by his or her daily eating habits, help change them. Introduce new, more nutritious foods to his or her diet by preparing them in fun ways, such as pancakes with fruit faces or sandwiches shaped with cookie cutters. Invite your child to help choose the weekly menu.

If you feel your child does not get enough sleep, observe his or her daily behavior. You may need to set a permanent bedtime and stick to it. Or, if your child has a lot of energy at the end of the day, you may wish to encourage more physical activity during the day.

Other Health-Related Issues

A healthy child can learn. If your child has a health problem, even if it does not seem related to literacy tasks, learning can be affected. Even children with mild health problems sometimes experience anxiety that affects learning. If your child has any health considerations, be sure to provide an environment that promotes self-confidence and perseverance.

Expectations

Friends, relatives, and teachers significantly influence your child's literacy development. Your response to the following questions can provide insight into how you can positively influence your child's literacy development: *What are your expectations for your child's literacy development? Are you setting a good example? How do you communicate with your child?* Expecting too much or too little affects how your child learns to read, write, or perform any task.

Expecting Too Much

The issue of "expecting too much" is a major concern. Children need realistic, sensitive guidance—not pressure. Many parents are tempted to enroll their children in several extracurricular programs and push for perfection in each. Others impose strict schedules in hopes of their child attaining academic, social, or sport-related stardom. Avoid pressuring and planning for your child; instead, guide him or her to take responsibility and set goals for his or her own success. Use the following tips when helping your child set goals.

● Informally interview your child to find out about skills (academic or otherwise) he or she wants to develop.

● Have your child prioritize and list the skills that are most important to develop first.

● Ask your child to choose one or two skills from the top of the list and create and carry out a plan for developing those interests or skills.

Whatever your child's age, beware of the temptation to expect too much too soon, for then, your child may choose *not* to listen, think, speak, read, or write. Always be thoughtful of and realistic about your child's schedule, personal goals, and developmental level.

Expecting Too Little

Some adults expect too little from children, and in turn, the children expect little of themselves. Avoid the inclination to believe that your child is not smart enough or does not have the capacity to do better. Be sure not to let test scores or an opinion offered by a teacher, psychologist, or other professional prompt you to come to the conclusion that your child cannot learn. All children can learn; they just learn in different ways at different rates.

Your child needs to be aware that everyone processes information differently. Talk it over together to help your child discover his or her own way. Your child will soon see that through perseverance, careful guidance from teachers, and your support, he or she *can* learn.

Balancing Expectations

How do you balance your expectations so you do not expect too much or too little? Sensitive observation and ongoing communication are important. Watch as your child plays and participates in daily activities. How does he or she respond to experiences that naturally involve thinking, listening, speaking, reading, and writing? A natural way to balance expectations is to observe your child's responses and set realistic literacy goals together.

Another way to create a balance is to be aware that your expectations and attitudes are reflected in your behavior. Set a good example at home by being positive, patient, inquisitive, self-disciplined, and eager to learn new things.

Communicate with other parents whose children are happy and learning. Do not seek out parents of only "overachievers." High-achievers are not necessarily happy. Struggling learners can be happy as they learn in their own way and at their own rate.

Discuss teaching and learning methods with your child's teacher, a learning specialist, or an administrator. No single educational approach is best for all children, so become informed and communicate with those who can help you find effective ways to help your child develop literacy.

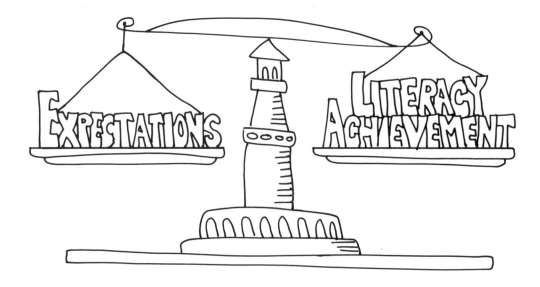

Educational Experiences and Resources

Your child's educational experiences, in and out of the classroom, influence his or her literacy development. Positive classroom experiences help your child take risks to learn. When your child relates well with the classroom teacher, he or she is more willing to think, speak, listen, read, and write. Encourage your child to become friendly with the teacher. Meet with your child's teacher to help him or her gain an understanding of what motivates and puts your child at ease. Explore the possibility of a parent/teacher/student conference. Show your child how you and the teacher are working as a team for his or her benefit.

Educational experiences often occur outside of the classroom. Positive everyday educational experiences such as family outings or watching and discussing an educational video, enhance literacy development as well. Make time for your child, and offer quality educational experiences like those explained on pages 21 to 107.

Educational Resources

The use of a variety of educational resources can greatly enhance literacy development. Almost anything in print can become an educational resource when used for a specific purpose. Restaurant menus are resources that can be easily obtained and used for literacy activities. Newspapers offer interesting articles, sports-related statistics, and funny comics to share with your child. Computers at school, in the library, or at home can be used to search for free or inexpensive activity books or meaningful literacy activities. (Pages 110–112 offer technology resources to use with the computer.) Even billboards and store signs can be used to help your child learn letters and words! Look around your house and environment and use whatever you have. Educational resources surround you.

Assessment experiences influence literacy success. How your child performs on a standardized test (and the teacher's or administrator's interpretation of the score) shape your child's curriculum and can qualify your child for a gifted program or special education.

Look beyond Test Scores

A wide variety of formal and informal tests and other performance tasks are administered to assess your child's literacy skills. Tests are designed for different purposes; for example, some assess individuals while others assess groups. Ask your child's teacher about standardized tests administered at your school (see below). In addition to learning about the tests, take time to look closely at your child's performance on everyday tasks so you can put test scores in perspective. Ask your child's teacher about "authentic" or "embedded" assessment—everyday tasks used to assess performance. In addition, ask if your child has a "portfolio" with work samples that show growth over time.

Ask Questions about Tests

Regardless of your child's age, ask the following questions about standardized tests. These questions help clarify, support, and verify your child's daily performance in comparison to his or her assessment experiences.

What is the full title and purpose of the test? Most standardized tests provide an overview of class or school performance, but few offer diagnostic information about individuals. Individually administered tests given by trained teachers or specialists have more potential for diagnosing your child's specific strengths and needs.

Which skills are tested? Reading vocabulary, comprehension, and spelling are examples of literacy skills or competencies often assessed on standardized tests. *All* test sections, including those in aptitude and I.Q. tests, require literacy skills. (For example, word problems in a *math* section require your child to be able to *read* or *listen* for comprehension.) When considering each test section, ask *What literacy skills are needed to perform well on this test?*

How are the skills tested? Vocabulary and word recognition are tested differently depending on test authors and publishers. For example, comprehension sections on some tests require your child to read brief passages and answer questions. Other tests assess comprehension by having your child fill the blanks in sentences without reading any passages. When considering a test section, ask *How closely does the section simulate skills applied in daily life?*

How does your child behave while taking a test? Your child's test-taking behavior can vary from day to day. He or she may feel tense and worried one day and relaxed and confident another. Hunger and fatigue can affect your child's performance. Keep these factors in mind when interpreting scores.

How are the scores determined, interpreted, and used? Norm-referenced and criterion-referenced (objective-referenced) tests are two types. Norm-referenced test scores reflect performance in comparison to a "norm-group"—a group of students similar in age and/or grade. Your child's score is compared to the "norm-group." Major test publishers compare students throughout the nation. In addition, these publishers may develop scores comparing your child's score to special "norm-groups." Find out which norm group is used to determine your child's score.

Your child's norm-referenced score may be reported as a percentile. Although many individuals think that percentiles represent the percentage of correct answers, they actually represent how your child ranks compared to other children in the "norm group" who took the test. For example, a fourth-grade student scoring in the 50th percentile on a nationally-normed test ranked better than 50% of the fourth-grade students participating in the national norm sample.

When considering scores on a norm-referenced test, be aware of the grade-equivalency score. Grade-equivalency scores are estimated comparisons, and do not specify a grade and month of actual performance. For example, a second grader who scored 5.1 (fifth grade, first month) on a norm-referenced test may be able to read words at that level, but may not have the background experience to understand fifth-grade reading content. Such a score indicates that, in comparison to other second graders in the "norm-group," this second grader did well.

ANY ACHIEVEMENT TEST

Teacher: Jones	1997 Norms:	MAT7 Spring
School: Waters Elementary	Grade: 02 Test Date: Level:	National Elem 1 National D
District: Any Community	03/97 Form:	S 1

INDIVIDUAL REPORT FOR A. STUDENT STUDENT NO. 000 AGE: 07 YRS. 01 MOS

TESTS	NO. OF ITEMS	RAW SCORE	SCALED SCORE	NAT'L PR-S	LOCAL PR-S	GRADE EQUIV	AAC RANGE	NATIONAL GRADE PERCENTILE BANDS
Total Reading	85	62	609	70-6	83-7	3.6	High	
Vocabulary	30	19	577	49-5	68-6	2.8	Middle	
Reading Comp.	55	43	628	78-7	88-7	4.7	High	
Total Mathematics	64	40	569	49.-5	58-5	2.8	Middle	
Concept & Problem Solving	40	25	573	47-5	54-5	2.7	Middle	
Procedures	24	15	560	50-5	64-6	2.8	Middle	
Language	54	28	578	45-5	62-6	2.5	Middle	
Prewriting	15	13	626	79-7	93-8	4.3	High	
Composing	15	2	515	5-2	4-2	0.3	Low	
Editing	24	13	588	55-5	73-6	3.0	Middle	
Science	35	29	643	92-8	96-9	5.7	High	
Social Studies	35	17	564	24-4	33-4	1.8	Low	
Research Skills	31	23	604	68-6	85-7	3.5	Middle	
Thinking Skills	78	54	600	66-6	81-7	3.5	Middle	
Basic Battery	203	130	589	56-5	73-6	3.0	Middle	
Complete Battery	273	176	590	57-5	73-6	3.0	Middle	

(Percentile band scale: 1 10 30 50 70 90 99)

Objective or criterion-referenced test scores reflect how your child meets the objectives (criteria) related to a specific skill. For example, reading criteria can assess how well your child predicts passage content, recalls details, and understands word meanings. Criterion-referenced tests are usually long because several questions are presented to test each objective within a skill area. Scores reflect how well your child meets the specified criteria. Some publishers offer norm-referenced and criterion-referenced scores for the same test.

Explore Different Approaches

Ability to function in the real world is the ultimate test. Some children are better test-takers than others. Some are less nervous, others more challenged, and still others see tests as games. With this in mind, explore how the teacher keeps a record of your child's performance on daily literacy tasks. For many teachers, performance records include audio- or videotapes of your child speaking and reading, unedited writing samples, a list of books that have been read, and individual or group projects. These performance records may give a more accurate view of your child's progress.

Because literacy is influenced by so many factors, it is important to work one-on-one with your child to positively influence development. Working one-on-one does not have to take a great amount of time or preparation; it simply takes a few minutes to do some fun, engaging activities. The following sections provide dozens of easy, exciting literacy activities to complete with your child. So start today! *You* can be the best and most effective literacy influence of all.

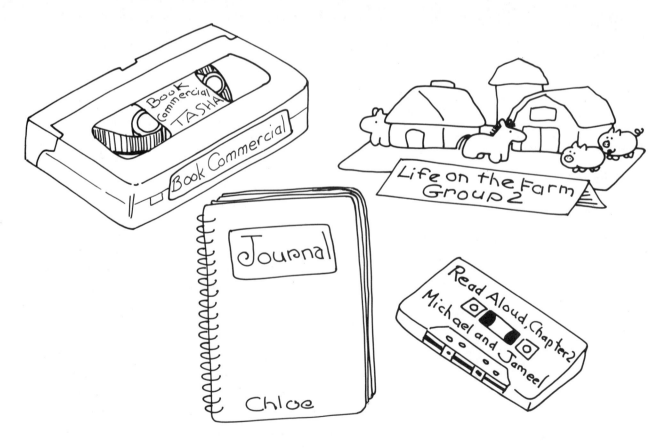

Hearing Sounds in Words

Can you hear the /c/ sound at the beginning of the word cat? How about the /t/ sound at the end of bat? If you can, you can hear sounds in words. Today's educators have a name for the ability to hear sounds in words— phonemic awareness. Hearing and using sounds begins when your child is an infant, and is the beginning of learning to speak, read, and write. Use the questions below to determine if your child needs to further develop his or her phonemic aware- ness. If you answer yes to one or more of the questions, help your child select activities from this section and com- plete them together. You'll have a sound-sational time!

DOES YOUR CHILD

- need you to repeat key words in a sentence to follow directions or understand a conversation?

- miss key words that make a conversation meaningful?

- struggle to clap to the rhythm in rhymes and songs?

- hesitate and seem reluctant to play action rhymes and games such as "Patty Cake" or "Simon Says"?

- struggle to repeat rhymes and poems?

- have difficulty making up new rhyming words by sub- stituting beginning letter sounds (such as *mat, hat, fat*)?

- have difficulty blending syllables heard in words while speaking (such as *chalk + board = chalkboard* or *hap + py = happy)*?

- have difficulty picking out beginning and ending sounds (such as sounds in the beginning and end of *fat* and *fan)*?

- have difficulty matching sounds heard in words (such as sounds that are the same in *fat* and *fan)*?

Lights, Camera, Action!

(Responding to Words through Actions)

MATERIALS

action songs, poems, nursery rhymes, or games

Here's a simple five-minute activity. Read aloud and act out the following action poem. Invite your child to watch the first time and then copy you as you read and act it out again. Practice the poem together many times until your child knows it "by heart."

My Garden	Motions
This is my garden. I'll rake it with care.	*Extend one hand forward. Make a raking motion on palm with other hand.*
Here are the flower seeds I'll plant in there.	*Make planting motions with thumb and index finger.*
The sun will shine and the rain will fall.	*Make a circle overhead with hands and then let fingers flutter down.*
And my garden will blossom and grow straight and tall.	*Cup hands together and extend slowly upward.*

Other action song or poem suggestions: "The Eeensy Weensy Spider," "Little Bunny Foo Foo," "Simon Says," "This Old Man," "One, Two, Buckle My Shoe," and "Patty Cake."

Drivin' to the Beat

(Hearing and Responding to Rhyming Sounds)

MATERIALS

children's songs or poems on cassette or compact disk

Have your child pick out favorite children's cassettes or compact disks from the library or store, or ask your child's teacher if you may borrow classroom cassettes or compact disks. Whenever you travel in the car, sing or recite the songs or poems. Add some excitement by singing or speaking rhyming words as loudly or softly as you can.

Clapping Machines
(Hearing and Responding to Rhythms)

MATERIALS
children's songs, poems, and raps on cassette or compact disk

Invite your child to pick out children's cassettes or compact disks from the library or store, or ask your child's teacher if you may borrow classroom cassettes or compact disks. Listen to the cassettes or compact disks with your child. Instead of singing or reciting, clap to the rhythm of the songs and poems together. Have a good time with it; you can even get up and dance while you clap! After becoming "clapping machines," sit down and talk about the importance of listening for the beat and trying to clap with it.

Can We Read It Again?
(Learning and Using New Letter-Sound Patterns)

MATERIALS
rhyming and alliterative stories, books, poems, magazine articles, or other reading materials

See the list below, or ask your child's teacher or a children's librarian for a list of reading materials that contain rhyme and alliteration (words that begin with the same letter). Read the materials to your child to discover his or her favorites. Whenever you hear *Can we read it again?*, reread the favorite selection and invite your child to "chime in" and read with you. Soon your child will be reciting words or passages from memory. Keep reading the favorites until your child is ready for new ones; then reread again!

Rhyming books: *Brown Bear, Brown Bear, What Do You See?* by Bill Martin, Jr.; *Chicken Soup with Rice* by Maurice Sendak; *Green Eggs and Ham* by Dr. Seuss; *The Napping House* by Audrey Wood; *A House Is a House for Me* by Mary Ann Hoberman; *The New Kid on the Block* by Jack Prelutsky; *Falling Up* by Shel Silverstein.

Alliterative books: *Q is for Duck* by Mary Elting and Michael Folsum; *Mike Mulligan and His Steam Shovel* by Virginia Lee Burton; *Tikki Tikki Tembo* by Arlene Mosel; *Animalia* by Graeme Base; *Comic and Curious Cats* by Angela Carter; *A Bundle of Beasts* by Patricia Hooper.

"Seeing" Sounds

(Identifying Letters or Groups of Letters by Their Sounds)

MATERIALS

everyday reading selection (menu, alphabet book, program from sporting or theatrical event)

This fun activity can take place anywhere! Ask your child to follow along as you read an everyday reading selection, pointing to key words. For example, when reading a menu, point to and read aloud food items from the children's menu. When reading an alphabet book, point to the letters as you come to them. When attending a sporting event or the theater, point out players' or performers' names in the program. Repeat this activity from time to time when you read an "everyday something" together. It will help your child make the sound/letter connection and give him or her an extra boost toward reading independently!

Take a Peek

(Seeing How Words We Say Are Written)

MATERIALS

paper
pencil or pen

Whenever you sit down to do some "real-world" writing, such as writing checks, filling out forms, making grocery lists, or writing phone messages, ask your child to watch you. Read aloud each word as you write. After writing, point out interesting word spellings or features. For example, if you wrote the word *cheese* on a grocery list, you might spell it aloud and point out that the last *e* is silent. Then you could ask your child to find other words in the list with a silent *e*. Have your child watch you write whenever you can; he or she will quickly make the connection between spoken sounds, reading, and writing.

Breaking Up Is Hard to Do

(Linking Letter Sounds and/or Syllables to Words)

MATERIALS

word list your child makes

Grab your child's attention by focusing on one of his or her interests, such as baseball, gardening, or animals. Invite your child to name words related to the interest. For example, if the interest is baseball, your child might say the words *bat, fun, champ, runner,* and *outfield.* Write the words on a list. Play Breaking Up is Hard to Do by saying each word, one sound at a time or one syllable at a time. Have your child guess the word you are "breaking up." For example, you might say each of the three sounds in the word *bat* (/b/ /a/ /t/), and then have your child guess *bat.* Other sound examples include /sp/ /or/ /t/ (sport), /f/ /u/ /n/ (fun), or /ch/ /a/ /m/ /p/ (champ). To divide words into syllables, you might say /pit/ /cher/ (pitcher) or /run/ /ner/ (runner). Play the game with each word. When your child wants to play again, use words from a different interest.

Tap Dancer

(Identifying Words in Sentences)

MATERIALS

everyday reading material (books, magazines, newspapers, nursery rhymes, poems)

Read aloud some everyday reading material. As you read a sentence or phrase, ask your child to stand and tap his or her foot as each word is read. Read the sentence or phrase a second time. Invite your child to tap again and count the number of words by counting aloud the taps. For example, if you read the phrase *And the cow jumped over the moon,* your child should tap seven times, one time as each word is read. When you read the phrase again, your child should say, *one, two, three, four, five, six, seven* as he or she taps. For extra fun, invite your child to get silly and think of funny ways to tap dance as you read.

Does It Fit?

(Distinguishing Same and Different Beginning or Ending Sounds)

MATERIALS

everyday reading materials (catalogs, magazines, newspapers, books, menus)

Need a surefire cure for a restless beginning reader? Review a catalog page, magazine or newspaper article, book page, or menu, and find two or three words that begin with the same sound, such as *shoe, shirt,* and *shorts.* Find another word that does *not* begin with the same sound, such as *belt.* Circle the words and read them aloud to your child. After reading, ask *Which word doesn't fit?* Have your child say the word. Repeat the activity with a group of words that have the same ending sound. Play Does It Fit? anytime, anywhere. With enough practice, your child will become a beginning- and ending-sound champion!

Silly Sounds

(Substituting Letter Sounds)

MATERIALS

funny rhymes or poems

Silliness is the name of the game with this fun activity. Read with your child a variety of funny rhymes and poems such as those by Jack Prelutsky or Shel Silverstein (see page 23 for a list). Ask your child's teacher or librarian or search the Web (see pages 110 to 112) for poetry and rhyme suggestions. After you read several poems aloud, choose words from the poems to "get silly with." Have your child get silly with the words. Have him or her add new beginning-letter or letter-combination sounds to make real *or nonsense* words such as *house, louse, pouse, shouse, fouse,* and *mouse.* Invite your child to list as many new words as possible for each word. To vary the game, play it on the road while driving and have your child make up new words from words on signs. By substituting letter sounds, your child gets to manipulate sounds, discover patterns in language, and have a good laugh with you!

The Alphabet

Learning the alphabet is one of the first steps to successful reading and writing. When your child can recognize letter shapes, names, and sounds, he or she develops dozens of skills, such as building words when writing, figuring out words when reading, and picturing words "in his or her head" when spelling. Use the questions below to determine if your child needs help learning the alphabet. If you answer yes to one or more of the questions, help your child select activities from this section and complete them together. They're as fun and easy as ABC!

DOES YOUR CHILD

- need help in recognizing upper- or lowercase letters?

- have difficulty remembering how some letters are written?

- need help in matching beginning letter sounds to letter names or shapes?

- have difficulty recognizing letters in order from *A* to *Z*?

- struggle to write letters out of alphabetical order?

- confuse letters having similar features, such as *b, d; p, q;* or *m, n,* and *w?*

- have trouble naming letters within words in real-world places such as in magazines or on billboards, signs, and menus?

- have trouble matching a beginning letter sound to an object whose name begins with that letter?

The Uppercase Alphabet

Cut out and use these cards (or other flash cards) for alphabet activities.

A	B	C
D	E	F
G	H	I
J	K	L
M	N	O
P	Q	R
S	T	U
V	W	X
Y	Z	

The Lowercase Alphabet

Cut out and use these cards (or other flash cards) for alphabet activities.

a	b	c
d	e	f
g	h	i
j	k	l
m	n	o
p	q	r
s	t	u
v	w	x
y	z	

ABC Book

(Recognizing Letter Shapes and Their Sounds)

MATERIALS

stapler or tape
blank paper
letter cards (pages 28 and 29)
crayons, markers
magazine pictures
scissors
glue

This fun activity can be completed in short, 10- to 15-minute sessions over several weeks. Staple or tape blank sheets of paper together to form a 26-page booklet. Help your child place the letter cards in alphabetical order on a table, grouping upper- and lowercase cards together to form pairs. Guide your child in copying or pasting copies of each pair of letters near the top of a book page. Choose a letter and book page. (Ask your child's teacher the order in which letters are introduced in school. Introduce letters in the alphabet book at the same time they are being introduced in school to reinforce learning.) Invite your child to cut out two or three magazine pictures that begin with the same sound as the chosen letter. For example, your child might cut out a flower and a flag for the letter *F*. Have your child glue the pictures on the book page. Continue with each letter of the alphabet in later sessions. When finished, invite your child to "read" the book to you. Your child might even like to read the book to the rest of the family, his or her class at school, or grandma and grandpa!

Beat the Clock

(Recognizing Upper- and Lowercase Letter Pairs)

MATERIALS

letter cards (pages 28 and 29)

timer or clock with a second hand

Short on time? Play Beat the Clock with your child for some split-second *ABC* fun. Review the names and shapes of five or six upper- and lowercase letter-card pairs by spreading the cards in order on a table and saying the name of each letter. Mix up the cards. Set a timer or watch a clock with a second hand, and challenge your child to match the cards as quickly as possible. Tell your child how long it took to match the cards. Play the game a few more times, and challenge your child to beat the original time. This is a very quick game , and your child will get some great practice with the alphabet.

Fun on Board

(Recognizing Letter Shapes)

MATERIALS

Turn riding in the car into quality alphabet time! While riding, look for the letter *A* on road signs, restaurants, license plates, billboards, or any word display. Point to and call out the letter when you see it. Invite your child to find the letter *B*. Continue the game through the entire alphabet, challenging passengers to find all letters before reaching your destination.

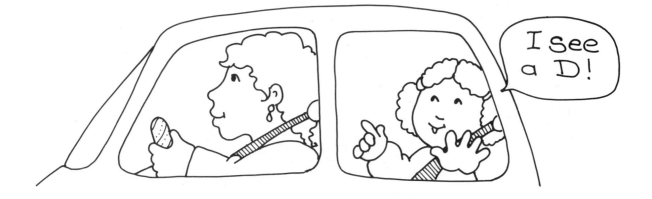

Make a Match

(Matching Upper- and Lowercase Letter Pairs)

MATERIALS

letter cards (pages 28 and 29)

Try a variation of "The Memory Game" with your child to give him or her some alphabet practice. Pick out five or six upper- and lowercase letter card pairs. (Choose three or four letters your child knows well and two or three that are new or challenging.) Lay the cards faceup in random order on the table. Invite your child to match the cards, offering help as needed. Turn the letter cards facedown in two columns with uppercase in the left column and lowercase in the right. Mix up the letters within each column. Ask your child to turn over one card from the left column and try to find the matching lowercase letter by turning a card over from the right column. If the upper- and lowercase letters do not match, have your child turn both cards facedown again. If the cards match, your child keeps the cards. Play until your child has all the pairs. If you want to play a second game together, challenge your child to make the matches more quickly or add more pairs to the columns.

Alpha

(Recognizing Letter Shapes and Names)

MATERIALS

Alpha card (page 33)

letter cards (pages 28 and 29)

markers (pebbles, pennies, paper squares)

It's Bingo with a twist! Make two Alpha cards, one for you and one for your child. Lay out all 52 letter cards so you and your child can see them. Write a different letter in each square of your Alpha card. Help your child do the same. Turn the cards facedown in a pile. Turn over the top card and ask your child to say the letter's name. Look for the letter on your Alpha card, and if it is there, place a marker over it. Have your child look for the letter on his or her card. Play the game until you or your child covers five letters across, vertically, or diagonally. The first person who covers five letters shouts *Alpha!* and wins the game!

Alpha Card

A	L	P	H	A
		Alpha Free Space		

Letter Art

(Relating Letter Shapes and Names to Objects)

MATERIALS

letter cards (pages 28 and 29)

crayons, markers

blank paper

glue

small disposable objects

Bring out the artist and reader in your child with this easy activity. Choose a letter of the alphabet. (Ask your child's teacher the order in which letters are introduced in school. Choose a letter that is currently being introduced.) Have your child look at the upper- and lowercase version of the letter and copy both in large print on a sheet of paper. Invite your child to search the kitchen and yard for small, disposable objects that begin with that letter such as sand for *S*, eggshells for *E*, leaves for *L*, or macaroni for *M*. Have your child cover the letters he or she wrote with glue and sprinkle the objects over the letters. When the letters dry, have your child trace over the letters with a finger and say the letter and object names. Display the artwork so the whole family can admire it.

In the Bag

(Relating Letter Sounds to Objects)

MATERIALS

letter cards (pages 28 and 29)

paper bag

tape

To begin this lively game, place either the upper- or lowercase alphabet cards in a paper bag. (You may wish to remove *X* from the bag because few objects begin with this letter.) Shake the bag, and invite your child to choose a letter from it. Say the letter sound for your child. Have your child search the house (as fast as he or she can) for an object that begins with that letter sound. For example, if your child chooses an *R*, he or she might run to the refrigerator. Have your child tape the letter to the found object and run back to the bag for another letter. Continue the game until all cards are taped around the house. For extra fun, have your child hop, crawl, skip, or gallop instead of run while looking for objects!

Recognizing Words

Congratulate your growing reader as he or she recognizes a word; it takes many problem solving skills! One way your child might "problem solve" to recognize a new word is by using context clues—clues such as real-world objects, pictures, or surrounding words in a sentence. Once your child "problem solves" and recognizes a new word, he or she can read it, understand its meaning, and write it! Use the questions below to determine if your child needs help in recognizing words. If you answer yes to one or more of the questions, help your child select activities from this section and complete them together.

DOES YOUR CHILD

- ignore picture clues as a way to recognize words?

- look quickly at a word when trying to read it, without taking time to focus on letters or sounds?

- ignore real-world objects that give clues to word names (such as the golden arches for McDonalds)?

- ignore other words in a sentence that should help in recognizing words?

- have difficulty recalling a word from memory by its shape (such as the shape of the word *tree*)?

- have difficulty recalling a word from memory by its similarity to another word (such as *meat* and *seat*)?

- have difficulty blending letter sounds, syllables, prefixes, suffixes, and other word parts to recognize words (such as "sounding out" the sounds /sp/ /or/ /t/ for *sport*)?

- struggle when reading or writing a new word, uncertain of how to meaningfully "unlock" it?

- begin to sound out a word but cannot "unlock" the rest of it?

Growing Strong
(Reading and Writing New Words)

MATERIALS
books
writing paper

Help your child see that he or she is growing into a strong reader with this simple activity. Observe your child's strengths as he or she reads and writes. Note and write down what your child does to figure out new words, such as:

● My child reads words before and after a new word to figure the new word out.

● My child relates new words to similarly spelled familiar words (such as *mail* and *pail*).

● My child uses picture clues to read a new word.

● My child says word parts out loud to read or write a new word.

Keep the strength list handy and consult it from time to time when your child is reading. Use one of the listed strengths to help your child read a new, difficult word.

Land on It!
(Recognizing Consonant Blends)

MATERIALS
blend grid (page 37)
penny
writing paper

Your child will "flip" for this fun game! Fill each square of the blend grid with a consonant blend such as *bl, br, cl, cr, dr, dw; fl, fr, gl, gr, pl, pr;* or *sl, sm, sn, sp, squ, st.* Review the grid with your child by saying each letter-combination sound aloud and naming a word that begins with that sound. To play, have your child toss a penny onto the grid and notice the consonant blend on which the penny lands. Read the blend aloud, and ask your child to name a word that begins with that blend. If your child cannot name a word, help out. After your child names a word, write it, read it, and have your child point out the consonant blend. Take a turn, and have your child read the combination for which you have to think of a word. Write your word down, read it, and again have your child point out the consonant blend. Continue play until both you and your child land on all letter combinations.

Blend Grid

Shake It and Make It

(Building New Words)

Avoid hearing *I'm bored!* by playing this fun make-a-word game. On each side of nine wooden cubes (found in craft stores), write a letter of the alphabet. Write the alphabet twice, plus two commonly used letters such as *T* and *R*. (If you have Boggle, you can use its cubes.) Place the cubes in a can. Have your child shake the can and dump out the cubes. Together, observe the letters facing up and use them in different combinations to create as many new words as possible. Help your child write (or you may keep a list of) the words and count them. Play as many times as you like and try to beat your previous scores; time will fly and your child will learn new words!

Shop 'Til You Drop

(Relating New Words to Real-World Objects)

Shop 'til you drop with this educational activity! When grocery shopping, point out and read words on signs, advertisements, and labels. For example, if you are in the produce section, you might point out and read the signs, *Bananas—$.59 a pound* and *Garden-Fresh Tomatoes*. Have your child point to the objects described by the words. For extra fun, play a food guessing game. Give your child a clue such as *I'm thinking of a vegetable that starts with the letter* C. Have your child guess until he or she names the food (carrot, cucumber, celery, etc.). When your child makes the correct guess, point to the word and invite your child to read it—it's food, it's fun, it's fantastic!

Word Speed-Up
(Developing Memory and Phonics Skills)

MATERIALS

list of school-related words
(from textbooks, spelling lists,
picture or nonfiction books)

small paper squares or cards

gameboard (page 40)

markers

writing paper

die

timer or watch with a
second hand

It's a race against the clock in this exciting word game. Help your child choose 12, 18, 24, or 36 school-related words and write each on a small paper square or card. Place each card facedown on a gameboard space, making an evenly numbered pile on each space. Have your child roll the die. Pick up all the words on that number space on the gameboard and set a timer (or begin to watch the clock) for five minutes. Have your child try to read each word. When your child successfully reads a word, give the word to your child. If he or she has difficulty, read the word aloud and put it back on the gameboard facedown. Have your child roll the die again after trying that pile and repeat the process, trying to read piles until time is up. Have your child count the words he or she read correctly. Review the missed words on the gameboard and put all the words back on the gameboard in different piles. If your child read all the words in five minutes, shorten the time to four minutes. If your child did not read the words in the given amount of time, lengthen the time to five and a half minutes. Play the game until all six piles have been read in the shortest amount of time.

Gameboard

1	2
3	**4**
5	**6**

Family Time Reading Fun © 1997 Creative Teaching Press

Seeing and Saying Key Words

(Linking Word Sounds to Letters)

MATERIALS

index cards

scissors

magazine cutouts

glue

thin-tip markers

small box or envelope

How can you help your child with phonics at home? Here is the answer! Each week, select one or two letter/sound combinations for your child to practice reading or writing. (Ask your child's teacher if you need help choosing combinations.) Letter/sound combinations could include

● single consonants (such as *b, p, d,* and *m*).

● consonant blends (such as *st, gl,* or *tr*).

● consonant digraphs (such as *ch, sh, th,* or *ph*).

● long and short vowels *(a, e, i, o, u)*.

● vowel combinations (such as *ea, ai, ee,* or *ie*).

● *r* combinations (such as *ar, er, ir, or,* or *ur*).

Review each letter combination and its sound. Help your child think of an object word that uses each combination and can be a reminder of the letter-sound combination. For example, if you are working on the consonant blend *bl,* your child might think of the word *blanket.* Write the word at the bottom of an index card, and underline the chosen letter combination. Have your child find a picture of the object from a magazine, cut it out, and glue it above the word on the card. Have your child make another card if you choose two combinations. Display the card(s) where your child can see it (them) when reading or writing. When reading or writing with your child, point to the card(s) as he or she attempts to read or write a new word that has the combination(s). If you are working on a vowel, use several cards to show various spellings that represent its sound. For example, for long *a,* your child might make cards for the words *tail, frame, sleigh,* and *tray.* When your child knows a combination, remove its card and store it in a small "reminder box" or envelope. Your child will love to see the cards go up, and come down!

Mystery Word
(Blending Letter Sounds)

MATERIALS

new-word word list from one subject or theme

markers

paper strips

book

Take a few minutes for some word fun! Here's just the activity. Make a list of five to ten short new words from one subject or theme. Write each word on the front of a paper strip, leaving a space between each letter or letter combination (such as *d-o-g*, *c-a-t*, or *c-ow*). Hide one strip in a book. Talk with your child about the "mystery word's" subject or theme. Gradually pull out the strip so your child sees the first letter or letter combination of the mystery word. Help him or her say the sound made by the letter or letter combination. Pull out the strip a little further so the next letter or letter combination shows. Help your child say that sound, and then blend it with the first one. Pull out the strip for the rest of the letters or combinations, and have your child say and blend each one. When the whole word is revealed, have your child blend all the sounds to read it. Play with each paper strip; your child will get some wonderful sound-blending practice!

Shopping for Words
(Identifying Words through Real-World Clues)

MATERIALS

writing paper

Need a good excuse to head for a shopping mall? How about helping your child learn to read? Before going to a mall, make a list of five to ten easily found words for your child to find while shopping. Words could include *exit*, *sale*, *Sears*, *men's*, *women's*, *today*, *escalator*, *elevator*, *shoes*, or *parking*. Read the list out loud, and give it to your child as you enter the mall. Challenge your child to find each word before you leave, and help out if needed. On your way home, congratulate your child on his or her success in shopping for words.

Understanding New Words

Recognizing words is only a beginning step in learning to read. Understanding words is the next step—this skill is linked to understanding sentences, paragraphs, and entire stories. Understanding stories is true reading, and it starts with understanding the meaning of individual words. Use the questions below to determine if your child needs help understanding words. If you answer yes to one or more of the questions, help your child select activities from this section and complete them together. Your child will soon be on the road to true reading!

DOES YOUR CHILD

- forget or not know meanings of common words when listening, speaking, reading, or writing?

- use few or repetitive words when communicating?

- seem afraid to use new words even after hearing or reading them?

- ignore picture clues to find the meanings of words?

- read a word that does not match the word in a sentence or picture?

- look quickly at a word when trying to read it, without taking time to focus on its meaning?

- ignore real-world objects that give clues to word meanings?

- ignore other words in a sentence that could help in recognizing word meanings?

Child Chat

(Hearing, Understanding, and Using New Words)

MATERIALS
none

It's so easy! Every day, take 10 to 15 minutes to talk with your child one-on-one. Discussions can take place in the car, at the dinner table—anywhere. Vary topics of discussion and introduce new words often. Topics could include sports, current events, geography, hobbies, family news, or your occupation. To start discussions, ask questions such as *Who is your favorite NFL team? Why?; What do you think about those tornadoes that hit Texas?;* or *If you could visit anywhere, where would you want to go?* During the discussion, ask questions such as *Do you agree with me? Why or why not?; What do you think about it?; Do kids think differently than adults about that subject? How?;* or *What would you do if you were in my situation?* Listen carefully and make eye contact. Show you value your child's opinions and ideas. A little chat will go a long way as your child begins to understand words when reading and writing!

Together Time

(Hearing and Understanding New Words in Context)

MATERIALS
chapter or picture books
other literature (letters, articles, road signs, music lyrics, cereal boxes, recipes)

Reading aloud to your child is a great "togetherness" activity. Whenever you can, choose a read-aloud place, time, and book. Introduce the book and discuss the title, author, illustrator, and cover. If you are reading a picture book, look at and talk about the pictures before reading it. Then read the whole story without interruption. For a chapter book, read aloud for at least ten minutes or long enough for the story to progress. This is a time for your child to listen and enjoy the story. Avoid asking questions. On days when you're short on time, read aloud and discuss words you see in letters, magazine articles, road signs, music lyrics, cereal boxes, and/or recipes. Remember, reading aloud is the best!

Draw a Word

(Understanding School-Related Vocabulary)

MATERIALS

school-related vocabulary
index cards
timer or clock with a
second hand
drawing paper
crayons, markers

Turn a spelling list, social studies lesson, or science glossary into a "work of art" with this exciting game. Write each word from a school-related subject on an index card. Place the cards facedown, in random order, in a pile. Gather two teams of at least two players. Choose one team to begin. Have a player from the first team choose a card and read it silently. Whisper the name and meaning of the word if the player needs help. Say *Go* and watch a timer or clock with a second hand. Have the player draw pictures to describe the word's *meaning* (not the word's spelling). For example, if the word is *ocean,* the "artist" might draw waves. Members of the artist's team call out guesses for the word. When a team member calls out the correct word, note the time lapsed and record it. Invite the second team to choose an artist and take a turn. Continue play until all words are guessed. Add each team's total time lapsed. The team with the smallest number wins.

Play-by-Play

(Learning and Using New Words in Context)

MATERIALS

It's so simple, yet so effective! After a special event, such as a football or soccer game, movie, or party, ask your child give a play-by-play to tell what happened. For example, if your child went to a birthday party, he or she might say *First we played Pin the Tail on the Donkey. Then we ate chocolate cake. Then Sarah opened her presents. Then we went home.* When situations are difficult for your child to describe, offer new words to fill the gaps or ask *What happened first, next…?* Offer more difficult vocabulary when your child uses simple or common words in his or her play-by-play. Respond to your child's ideas with interest. Use new words in your response. Ask, *Did I use any words that were new to you? Which ones? What do you think each word means?* Explain the meaning of each word if necessary. As your child becomes better and better at the "play-by-play," invite him or her to speed up the commentary, just like real sportscasters.

Cleaning Day Fun

(Connecting Words and Their Meanings)

MATERIALS

children's everyday items (clothing, toys, sports equipment, art supplies)
storage units (dressers, shelves, milk crates, cardboard boxes)
file folder labels
thin-tip markers

Cleaning and learning can happen with this fun, educational activity! On housecleaning day, gather a pile of your child's clothing, toys, sports equipment, or art supplies. Help your child sort the items into several categories, such as socks, underwear, pants, and shirts for the category *clothing*. Ask your child to name each item and the category in which the item belongs. Have your child choose storage units such as drawers or shelves for the categories. Help your child write the name of each category on a file folder label and place it on its designated storage unit. Have your child store the items. Once a month, help your child go through the storage units to see that items are correctly placed.

Q and A Time

(Improving Verbal Communication)

MATERIALS

Instead of get-no-answer questions such as *How was your day?* or *What did you learn in school today?,* ask questions that encourage your child to think and use new words. Ask questions such as *What did you do that made today so much fun?; What did you see in the movie that made it a comedy, a mystery, or an adventure?; What was the easiest lesson you had in school today? What does _____ do that is special as your best friend?* or *What would you like to do this summer?* If your child gives answers that use few words (such as *It was fun*), help out by suggesting new, more interesting words. If your child likes to take the easy way out and give answers such as *Nothing, I don't know,* or *No,* you could share something from your own experience about school, summer activities, friendship . . . and ask how your experience or opinions are the same or different from your child's. This "modeling" can give your child some ideas. When you show you are interested by asking questions, your child will become more interested and learn new words at the same time!

Picture What You Mean!

(Matching Words to Picture Definitions)

MATERIALS
index cards
markers

It's word fun for everyone when you play Picture What You Mean! Make five to ten new word/definition card pairs. Write words on half the cards and their picture definitions on the other cards. For example, you might make one card with the word *house* on it and on a matching card draw a picture of a house. Place the cards faceup and help your child put pairs together. Turn the cards facedown, mix them up, and place them in rows. Invite your child to turn over two cards, one at a time. Have him or her say the word and/or definition revealed. If your child turns over a match, invite him or her to keep the cards. (Your child can take an extra turn for each match.) If your child does not turn over a matching pair, turn the cards facedown again. Remind your child to remember where words and definitions are to make a match the next time. Take turns until all matches are made. For extra fun, invite your child to make cards from new words for you to match; your child will learn twice the words!

Computer Fun

(Learning Word Meanings through Computer Tools)

MATERIALS
picture book
writing paper
computer
word-processing software
with a thesaurus and
dictionary

Hop on the information superhighway with your child and watch him or her speed into reading! Read a picture book aloud to your child. After reading, invite your child to choose four or five unfamiliar words and list them. Show your child how to look up one word in a computer's thesaurus. (If you do not own a computer, use the library's or ask the teacher if you and your child can spend a few minutes after school.) Read the list of synonyms aloud. Ask your child if he or she now understands the new word's meaning. If your child does not understand the new word, look it up in the computer's dictionary. Read the definition aloud and invite your child to use the new word in a sentence. Continue with each new word. If you have time, invite your child to write a sentence for each word on the computer and print them out. Have fun with the words; make graphics for them, look them up as subjects on the Internet, or just have your child type them. The more you do, the more your child will learn!

Wish Lists

(Relating New Words to Real-World Objects)

MATERIALS

catalogs, newspapers, or magazine advertisements

scissors

glue

blank paper

Want to keep your child busy for hours just before a holiday or birthday? Try this! Invite your child to cut out and glue pictures from catalogs or advertisements to form a "wish list"—a list of gifts he or she wants that fit a certain budget or other expectation. Have your child describe each object by writing its name and a short description near the picture that describes how it would be used or how it meets the expectations. When you have your child make "wish lists," your child can stay occupied during an otherwise excitable time and learn, all at once!

Word Search in Reverse

(Learning Word Spellings and Definitions)

MATERIALS

word list (from a text-book, spelling list, or literature selection)

writing paper

word search grid (page 49)

It's a word search in reverse; your child writes it, someone else solves it! Have your child make a list of five or six words from a textbook, spelling list, or literature selection. Show how to place the words on the word search grid horizontally, vertically, or diagonally. Have your child write random letters in the empty squares to hide the chosen words. Invite your child to give the word search to a family member. Instead of having the family member search for words right away, ask your child to choose a word and tell only its meaning. Challenge the family member to guess the word. Have your child give clues until the word is guessed. Then have the family member search for the word and circle it. Invite your child and the family member to play the game until all words are found.

Word Search Grid

Hide and Guess
(Using Descriptive Language)

MATERIALS
paper bag
small object

What's the opposite of Show and Tell? It's Hide and Guess; and it's lots of fun and builds an understanding of new words! Hide a small object, such as a pinecone, in a paper bag. Gather the family or your child's friends. Ask your child to give clues that describe what the object looks like, how it is used, and how it feels when touched. For a pinecone, clues might include *The object is as long as a crayon. It grows on trees. It's prickly and brown.* Help your child give clues by asking questions such as *What is the object's size? What color is it?* or *Where can you find the object?* Invite family members or friends to guess the object's name. Play the game again in two to three weeks. Challenge your child to use "better words" (more detailed descriptions) and lessen the number of clues needed or reverse roles. You can set an example by giving challenging clues with new descriptive words.

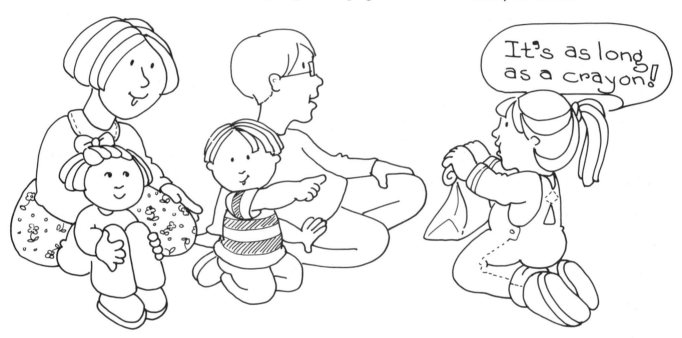

Definition Dictionary
(Building Word Recognition and Understanding)

MATERIALS
stapler or tape
blank paper
books or magazine or news articles
crayons, markers (optional)
magazine cutouts (optional)
scissors (optional)
glue (optional)

This activity is just what your child needs to recognize and remember new words. Invite your child to choose a personal interest (such as sports, music, or games), a topic (such as science, math, or social studies), or a special day (such as Valentine's Day or a birthday). Use your child's choice as the theme for a dictionary. Staple or tape blank sheets of paper together to form a 26-page book. Have your child write a letter of the alphabet at the top of each page. Read an interest/topic-related book or article aloud to your child. Invite him or her to choose five unfamiliar words from the reading. Help your child write each word on the book page that matches the beginning letter of the word.

Discuss the words' definitions and help your child record them next to the words by drawing pictures, gluing on magazine cutouts, or writing sentences or key words. Keep working together on the theme until the book is full or your child chooses another theme.

Listening & Reading Comprehension

Deriving meaning from words we hear and see in print is called comprehension—and it's the ultimate goal of listening and reading. To develop the skills to comprehend, your child needs to use past experiences; use listening and reading every day; and have the ability to predict before, interact during, and react after listening and reading. Use the questions below to determine if your child needs help with listening and reading comprehension. If you answer yes to one or more of the questions, help your child select activities from this section and complete them together.

DOES YOUR CHILD

- need help predicting what will be heard or read before and during listening or reading?

- fail to see a purpose for listening to or reading a specific piece of literature?

- seem distracted and disinterested while listening or reading?

- have difficulty sharing ideas about what has been heard or read?

- fail to smile, laugh, or react while listening to funny poems, jokes, or stories?

- have trouble following written or spoken directions?

- fail to respond to words in print naturally or have opinions about them unless asked?

- have difficulty remembering or retelling what is read or heard?

Go and Know

(Gaining Background Knowledge)

MATERIALS
books or children's magazines

The more you and your child go, the more your child will know! To help your child "go and know," ask him or her to choose a favorite subject such as animals, insects, dinosaurs, or space. Pick out two or three books or magazine articles about the subject from the library or bookstore. Review the books or articles before your child sees them, and brainstorm places to visit together that provide information about the subject. For example, if you choose animal books, you might visit a zoo, farm, nature preserve, or animal shelter. Visit one or two places with your child *before* reading. During the visits, discuss points of interest and your child's observations. Back at home, invite your child to tell everything he or she knows about the subject and make predictions about the books or articles based on information from the visits. Read and discuss the books or articles with your child. Throughout the year, complete Go and Know with your child to broaden his or her knowledge of the real world. . . and the world of print!

Reading Is Everywhere!

(Understanding that Reading and Listening Have a Purpose)

MATERIALS
several types of literature (magazine articles, music lyrics, recipes, game or toy operation manuals, birthday cards, letters)

This one's as easy as placing a few things around the house ..... Invite your child to name his or her interests and hobbies such as playing a sport, cooking, playing an instrument, or using the computer. Gather several literature examples about your child's interests. Display the literature everywhere—in the bathroom, on coffee tables, in the car, on dressers, and on bookshelves. Invite your child to read the literature alone and with you. Discuss the literature together and with the family. Change the literature as your child's interests change. Your child will soon see that reading is everywhere!

Take a Wild Guess

(Predicting)

MATERIALS
picture book

Before "digging in" to a book for the first time, invite your child to take a wild guess! Choose a book new to your child. Become familiar with its characters, setting, and plot. With your child, read the title, author, and illustrator and talk about the cover illustration. Ask your child to guess what the story will be about, just by looking at the cover. Look at the pictures on each page. Discuss the characters, setting, and plot, and ask your child to guess what will happen in the story. Read the book together. Invite your child to change his or her guesses or share correct guesses as you read. Invite your child to guess each time you read a new book together, and remind him or her to do the same when reading alone. When your child guesses before reading, he or she will spend a lot less time figuring out words and ideas during reading; it pays to take a wild guess!

Show It When You Know It

(Showing Understanding)

MATERIALS

picture book
props (optional)
writing or drawing supplies
(optional)
magazine cutouts (optional)
scissors (optional)
glue (optional)

All this activity requires is a good book and a little imagination! Invite your child to choose a special way of sharing a story, such as acting, writing a poem or song, telling, drawing, or making a collage of magazine cutouts. Read a book together. Invite your child to retell the story in order in his or her own special way. Help out if your child forgets or confuses characters or the order of events. If your child makes a drawing or collage, have him or her tell you about it. Invite your child to retell stories in different ways throughout the year. Your child may even discover a new talent along the way!

Hear It First

(Improving Reading Comprehension through Listening)

MATERIALS

any textbook or storybook passage

Sometimes a little exposure to a story in advance is all it takes for your child to understand. Use Hear It First when your child is reading a passage with new or challenging ideas. Invite your child to read the title of the passage (if it has one) aloud. Discuss the title. Read the passage *to* your child and let him or her listen. Ask your child to read the passage silently for a second "round" and then aloud to you. Discuss the passage, and ask your child to tell what he or she has heard and read to discover what your child understands. After gathering information in three different ways, your child has a greater opportunity to understand!

Leave It Out

(Predicting)

MATERIALS

picture book, magazine article, poem, or nursery rhyme

While reading aloud a picture book, article, poem, or nursery rhyme in which words and ideas are easy to predict, leave out a word or words in each sentence or stanza. (For example, if you read *The horse ran from the barn,* you might leave out the word *barn.)* Invite your child to suggest a word or words. If he or she suggests words that do not change the meaning of the sentence or stanza, keep going. If your child suggests words that don't make sense, stop reading and help him or her use picture clues or sound out words to come to a meaningful answer. Play Leave It Out from time to time to help your child think about meaning while reading.

I Can Read It and Do It!

(Understanding a Purpose for Reading)

Choose a special project to complete together such as building a model, completing a science experiment, following a recipe, putting together a toy, or making a craft. Have your child read the directions for each step independently or listen to them as you read them aloud. Invite your child to follow each direction after you read it. If your child does not follow a direction correctly, read the direction again. Offer help as needed. Display the project and let family members know how proud you are. Here's a simple recipe to get you started!

SUPER SNACK

1. Place 2 cups popcorn in a large bowl.
2. Add 1/3 cup small pretzels, 1 tablespoon shelled peanuts, and 1/4 cup animal crackers.
3. Stir in 1/8 teaspoon powdered butter and a pinch of salt.
4. Stir the super snack.
5. Eat it up!

It's Fun to Organize

(Organizing and Communicating Ideas)

Help your child organize his or her thoughts after reading with these few easy steps. Choose a story, nonfiction passage, or poem to read with your child. Make a copy of or draw an organizer (Story Map, I Know Grid, or Poetry Flower) from pages 56 through 58. Set the organizer aside. Invite your child to listen as you read the text aloud, or have him or her read to you. After reading, help your child recall ideas by filling in the organizer. If your child has trouble remembering, go back and reread sections of the text to find the answers. (Extension: Organizers can also be used when your child has a writing assignment. Invite your child to use an organizer *before* writing to develop a meaningful writing plan.)

Story Map

(Organizer for a Story/Picture Book)

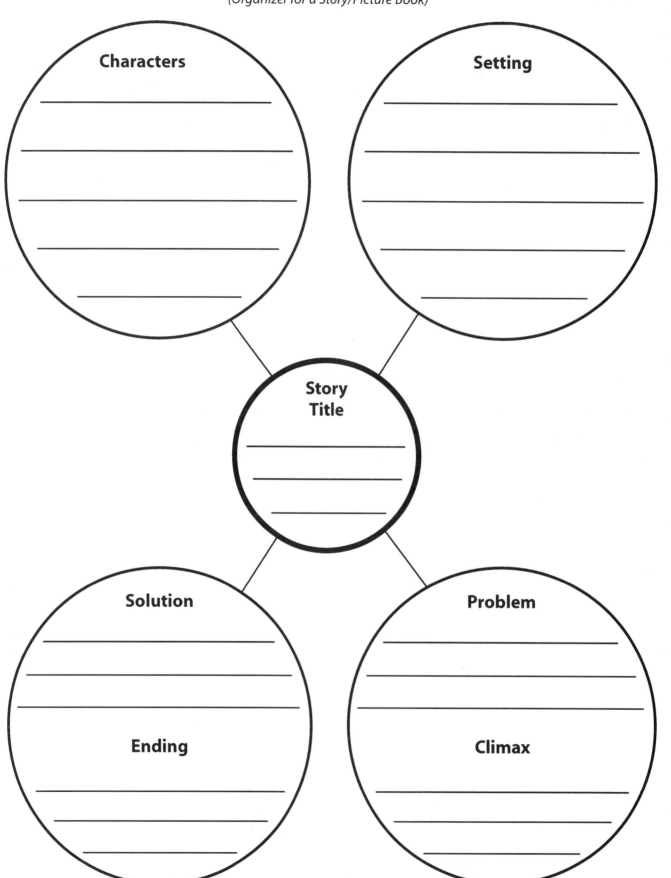

Family Time Reading Fun © 1997 Creative Teaching Press

I Know Grid

(Organizer for Nonfiction)

Before I Read I Thought	**Now I Know**

Five Things I Learned	**Now I Want to Know**
1.	
2.	
3.	
4.	
5.	

Hide and Guess

(Organizer for Poetry)

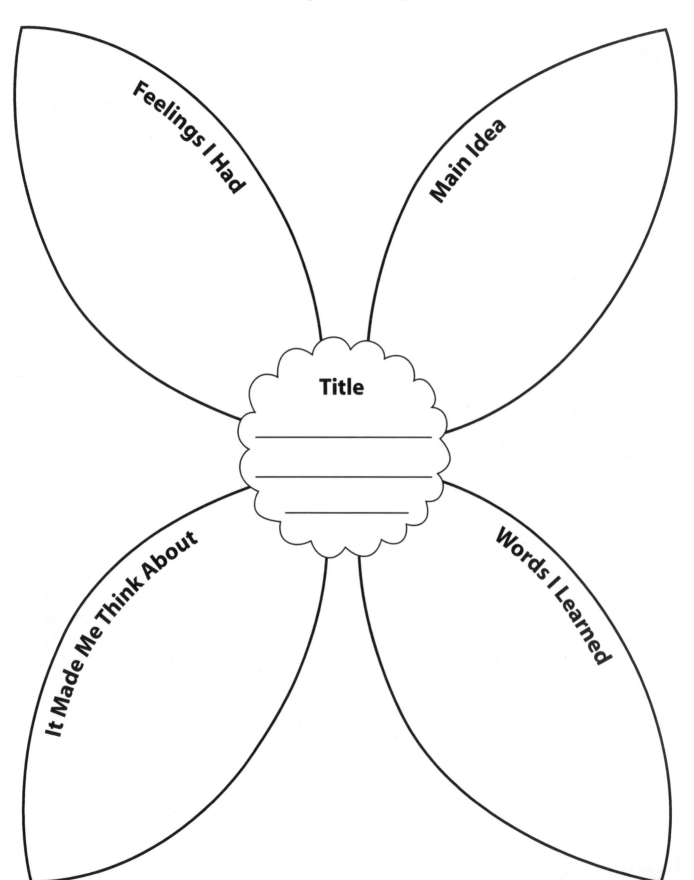

Feelings I Had

Main Idea

Title

_____

_____

_____

It Made Me Think About

Words I Learned

Family Time Reading Fun © 1997 Creative Teaching Press

Laugh It Up

(Demonstrating Comprehension)

MATERIALS
funny stories, poems, or articles

Laughter is a great way to check on comprehension. Select funny stories, poems, or articles. Invite your child to listen or read. Watch—does your child laugh or smile? Laugh it up with your child and explain what you thought was funny. With time, as your child becomes better at listening and reading, he or she will laugh or smile without your prompting; then you will know he or she really understands what is heard or read.

Is It Too Hard?

(Choosing Books at the Correct Reading Level)

MATERIALS
books

Do you ever find yourself asking *Is that book too hard for my child to read alone?* You can quickly answer that question by trying one or more of these easy strategies.

● Observe your child reading alone. If your child seems frustrated because the text has too many words or pages, suggest materials with fewer.

● If your child has a vision or confidence problem, suggest books with larger print or less print on a page.

● "Fingers On/Fingers Off Test": Test text by having your child read aloud approximately 50 words from the book he or she wants to read. Have your child place a finger on the bottom of the page for each word he or she struggles to read. If your child puts less than five fingers down, he or she is "ready to roll" and can probably read the book alone. If your child puts five or more fingers down, the book is probably too difficult. (But don't abandon that difficult book! Your child can still enjoy it when you read it aloud.)

Picture It
(Improving Listening Comprehension)

MATERIALS
picture book

It's easy, it's fun, it's Hide and Seek with books! Read a picture book aloud to your child, but do not show the pictures. Instead, encourage your child to "make pictures in his or her head" to visualize the story. Read the story a second time, and stop after each page. Invite your child to describe each imagined picture. Show each illustration, and compare your child's visualization to the actual illustration. At the end of the story, discuss how the illustrations add to the story's meaning and offer clues for understanding words.

Fill in the Blanks
(Making Meaning Using Context Clues)

MATERIALS
note to
your child

When you have a few minutes for some writing and reading fun, try this activity. Write two identical notes to your child, one with all the words, and one that leaves out several "key words." Write "fill-in-the-blank" lines for key words. Have your child read or listen to the fill-in-the-blank note and suggest words to fill the blanks. Remind him or her that the words should make sense, but do not have to match the original note. Have fun with the notes; invite your child to make funny or silly suggestions. Read your child's note and then the original aloud. Discuss and compare both. As you play Fill in the Blanks on other days, vary the subject of the notes. You can write thank-you notes, love notes, reminders, or just about anything!

Before, During, and After

(Thinking about Meaning)

MATERIALS
picture book or children's magazine article

Instead of speeding through a picture book with your child, take a few minutes to ask questions before, during, and after the reading. Avoid "yes or no" questions; ask questions that have your child think, predict, and draw conclusions. Ask questions such as

- *What do you think this story/article will be about? Why?*
- *Will this be a funny, sad, or scary story/article? How do you know?*
- *What do you think will happen next?*
- *What is your favorite part of the story/article?*
- *Which character did you like most? least? Why?*
- *Who was telling the story/article? How do you know?*
- *Was there anything in the story/article you didn't understand? What?*

Ask questions during natural breaks in the story. If a story is getting exciting, keep on reading. Ask questions to enrich meaning while reading; pretty soon your child will be doing it on his or her own!

Playing Secretary

(Communicating Comprehension)

MATERIALS
picture book
drawing paper
crayons, markers

"Language experience" is a name educators use for "playing secretary" by taking dictation from children. Teachers play secretary all the time to help students communicate their ideas. And you can do it at home with your child simply by reading a picture book aloud or talking about a recent experience. Afterward, ask *What happened?* On the top of a piece of drawing paper, write your child's answer word-for-word. (Do not change words or shorten sentences.) Read the answer aloud. Invite your child to read it to you. You will be amazed at how well he or she reads! Have him or her illustrate below the words. Display your child's work, and have him or her read it to you whenever he or she wishes.

Sentence Scramble

(Creating Meaning from Words)

MATERIALS
picture book
index cards
markers

This game is easier than making scrambled eggs! Read a picture book aloud. Choose two or three important sentences from the book. Write each word from the sentences on an index card. Capitalize and use other correct punctuation when writing words. Place one sentence in order on the table. Help your child read it. Scramble the cards so the sentence is out of order. Ask your child to unscramble the words to form a sentence. Repeat the activity with other sentences. As your child becomes better at unscrambling sentences, make the activity more challenging by adding new words to original sentences or by choosing longer sentences. If your child likes a little competition, record the time it takes to unscramble a sentence and challenge him or her to unscramble a new sentence more quickly.

Stump the Grown-Up

(Asking and Answering Questions)

MATERIALS
picture book

Read a picture book aloud, or have your child read it to you. Invite your child to take two or three minutes to think of questions to ask you about the story. Challenge your child to try to "stump" you. Then it's your turn. Ask your child two or three questions about the story. Help your child find the answers in the book (through rereading, using picture clues, or looking through the pages to remember story sequence) if he or she does not know the answer. Take turns asking and answering questions. Watch out, after a few times playing this game, your child might become a terrific "question asker" and actually stump the grown-up!

Fluency

When speaking, reading, and writing, your child's ideas need to "flow" and be communicated to others so ideas are understood. In other words, your child needs to be fluent. Fluency means speaking, reading, and writing with expression, a natural flow, and a meaningful pace. Use the questions below to determine if your child needs help with fluency. If you answer yes to one or more of the questions, help your child select activities from this section and complete them together. With a little help, your child's ideas will "flow" in no time!

DOES YOUR CHILD

- lack confidence when speaking, reading aloud, or writing?

- not seem to know why he or she is reading something aloud or writing?

- speak and read aloud without expression?

- lack a natural flow when reading aloud, using "choppy" speech?

- hesitate when speaking, reading aloud, or writing?

- have trouble recalling what he or she reads aloud because of uneven speech patterns?

- write sentences that seem unnatural or unconnected to each other?

Tape It

(Hearing Fluency in Reading)

MATERIALS

picture book
cassette recorder
blank cassettes
videotaped/audiotaped
book readings
(optional)

An easy way to help your child hear the difference between fluent and nonfluent reading is to read aloud to him or her. To demonstrate how fluent reading sounds, tape-record yourself reading aloud from a picture book. Use expression and read in a natural, evenly paced way. Invite your child to listen to the recording and follow along in the book. After listening, discuss fluency with your child. Encourage your child to listen to more fluent reading by tape-recording other stories or by purchasing or checking out from the library videotaped or audiotaped books. As you listen together, comment on the reader's expression and fluency skills. Through listening, reading fluency for your child can be just around the corner!

Check, Please!

(Becoming a Confident Speaker)

MATERIALS

Try this fun activity if your child is shy or needs a little practice speaking fluently in public. On an errand-running trip with your child, ask him or her to be your "voice." Have your child order food at a restaurant, ask where an item is located at a store, ask about a price at a checkout stand, or ask for directions in a mall. Encourage your child, and help when needed. At the end of the trip, congratulate your child on a job well-spoken!

Echo Reading

(Reading and Speaking with Expression)

MATERIALS

poem, limerick, or joke

Bring out the actor (and fluent reader) in your child with the following simple activity. Explain that reading is more exciting to listen to when the reader changes his or her voice to show feelings, just like an actor. Choose a poem, limerick, or joke to read aloud, such as

Knock, Knock!

Who's there?

Gorilla!

Gorilla, who?

Gorilla me a hamburger please!

Read one sentence/stanza at a time with expression. Ask your child to read after you as your echo. Encourage your child to use the same kind of voice. Remind him or her to read with the same expression when reading alone.

More Fun than One

(Reading and Speaking Smoothly with Expression)

MATERIALS

choral reading material (music lyrics, play dialogue, poems)

This activity proves that two can be more fun than one! Explain that some literature is meant to be read (or sung) by several people at once so it sounds like one voice (choral reading). Invite your child to brainstorm times when he or she has seen or heard several people sounding like one voice. Have your child listen to or read choral reading materials such as music lyrics (found inside cassette-tape or compact-disk packages), plays, or poems for groups. Invite your child to choose one choral reading to read aloud with you. Practice reading until you sound like one voice. Choose a special time and date, and perform your choral reading for family or friends. Encourage the rest of the family to perform the next choral reading with your child. The practice will be great for your child's fluency and your family's togetherness.

Joking Around
(Speaking and Reading with Expression)

MATERIALS
joke book
table
blanket
two puppets

This activity will tickle your child's funny bone! Help your child choose several lively jokes from a joke book. Set up a puppet stage by covering a table with a blanket. Wear one puppet and have your child wear another. Have your child practice telling the jokes using his or her puppet. Help with the jokes by having your puppet make comments such as *I don't know, What?*, or *How ____ was it?* Encourage your child to memorize the words and really "ham it up." Perform the jokes together for family members.

News Reporter
(Writing, Reading, and Speaking Naturally)

MATERIALS
writing paper
posterboard
tape
table
video recorder
(optional)

Have your child name family and school events and choose two to become news reports. Write down your child's reports, word for word, and read them back to him or her. Help your child change the reports so they sound like news. Record the finished reports on posterboard to make TelePrompTers, and tape them on the wall near a table. Have your child sit at the table and read from the TelePrompTers. Encourage him or her to read clearly and smoothly with expression. Gather the family for the "broadcast." If you have a video recorder, videotape your child as he or she gives the news. For extra fun, have your child make the report just before a holiday, and send the tape to relatives as a gift or family newsletter!

Catalog Letter

(Writing in a Natural "Voice")

MATERIALS

clothing and toy catalogs
writing paper

Before a special gift-giving event, invite your child to look through catalogs to choose one thing he or she would like. Invite your child to write you a brief letter asking for the item. Tell your child that the letter should be written in his or her own "voice" and should sound comfortable, like he or she is talking, not "stiff" or formal. Write the date and *Dear _____,* at the top of the paper. Have your child dictate the letter to you. Write down everything word-for-word. Do not change words or interrupt the natural flow of your child's speech. Close the letter with *Love, _____.* Read the letter back with expression. Ask your child to read it, with a reminder that you will be more convinced if your child reads the letter like he or she means it. From time to time, invite your child to write, instead of speak, when asking for things; your child will get great writing practice, and you'll get a special memory of your child's wishes to save.

Going to the Doctor

(Speaking Confidently with Purpose)

MATERIALS

Before visiting the doctor or dentist, invite your child to do most of the talking. Prepare your child by asking questions that the doctor or dentist might ask such as *Where does it hurt?; How are you feeling today?; What brings you here today?; How did you hurt yourself?;* and *How long have you been feeling this way?* Help your child think of accurate, descriptive answers. At the office, tell the doctor or dentist that your child would like to do the talking today. Feel free to "chime in" when your child needs help explaining something. Besides getting fluency practice, your child will learn to give accurate, detailed answers. Now that's what the doctor ordered!

Say it Like You Mean It
(Practicing Voice Inflection)

MATERIALS
none

Have some fluency fun with phrases you hear every day such as *I'm hungry; May I have some more?; May I be excused?;* or *You promised.* Ask your child to choose a phrase and say it three different ways. First, have your child say it like a question. Then have your child say it happily or excited. Finally, have your child say it angrily. Encourage your child to really "ham it up."

Have your child repeat the activity with two other phrases. Discuss how the same phrase can change meaning depending on the type of voice used. Explain that your child should think about words he or she says or reads aloud to make sure he or she is saying them the right way. When you're done, invite your child to use his or her best expression and shout *Hooray!*

Story Words
(Thinking to Make Speech Smooth and Natural)

MATERIALS
index cards
markers
paper bag
tape recorder
(optional)

Here is a game that changes every time you play it! Help your child think of several nouns (people, places, things). The nouns can be real (such as *fish*) or imaginary (such as *dragon*). Write each word on an individual index card. Place the cards in a paper bag, and have your child choose three. Read the cards with your child. Explain that he or she has two minutes to think of a story that includes those three words. Challenge your child to think (and not speak) for two minutes. Explain that if he or she thinks of a story before time is up, the extra time can be spent practicing the story "in his or her head." Invite your child to tell the story, helping if needed. Play again or keep the bag and play from time to time until all cards are chosen. (Optional: Tape-record the stories so your child can use the ideas for future writing.)

Taking Turns

(Speaking with Confidence Using Logical Vocabulary)

MATERIALS

It's sentence fun in the car, sentence fun on a walk, sentence fun at the table; it's sentence fun anywhere! Think of several sentence beginnings, such as

- *When I went shopping …*
- *My favorite memory is …*
- *I love …*
- *If I could have dinner with the president …*
- *When I was a baby …*
- *I can't wait to …*

Say the beginning of a sentence aloud, and invite your child to finish it. For example, if you say *My favorite memory is,* your child might say *when we went camping at the state park.* Encourage your child to use words that make sense and finish the sentence within ten seconds. Play until your child gets the hang of it and can complete sentences quickly and logically. Then invite your child to say sentence beginnings for you!

See Writing Grow

(Writing Smoothly and Confidently)

MATERIALS

picture book that gives a reader strong feelings
writing paper
clock
file folder

Read the picture book aloud. Ask your child to share feelings about it aloud and then in writing. Tell your child that he or she is to write as much as possible for five minutes without taking a break for spelling, rereading, or worrying. Invite your child to write about anything; there is no pressure to write the perfect paragraph. Say *Go.* Help your child focus by sitting next to him or her. After five minutes, have your child read the words back to you, and discuss the writing. Before ending, remind your child that, with practice and guidance, writing can become as natural as speaking. Ask your child to date what was written so you can save these "first drafts" in a file folder and watch writing grow over time. With a little practice, your child can get rid of writing "roadblocks" and "go with the flow" as he or she writes!

What a Character!

(Reading Aloud with Expression)

MATERIALS

familiar fairy tale or fable with dialogue (such as *Little Red Riding Hood*)

Invite your child to make a book come alive with this fun activity! Read a familiar fairy tale or fable aloud. For each character, use a different voice. Read the dialogue with a lot of expression. Before reading the story again, invite your child to choose a character. Have your child take that character's part and say the lines. Encourage your child to speak clearly and smoothly with expression as you read a second time together. If your child wishes, have him or her choose another character for another round of reading. Use this activity from time to time when you and your child read a book with fun or interesting characters.

The First Thing

(Brainstorming to Increase Vocabulary)

MATERIALS

writing paper
file folder

Your child will have a great time playing this simple, split-second-reaction game. Make a list of several household items such as *flower, coat, couch,* and *fence.* Read each word aloud, one at a time. Invite your child to write down the first word he or she thinks of upon hearing the word. For example, if your child hears the word *flower,* he or she might write *vase.* Encourage your child to think and write as quickly as possible. (If your child is a beginning writer, you can write the word as your child watches.) Discuss your child's answers and keep lists with dates to show how your child's knowledge of words is growing over time. Change the game each time you play it by choosing new word categories such as birthday words, holiday words, sports words, or food words; the possibilities are endless!

Forming Letters & Words

With a little help, your child can pick up a pencil and write words that are neat, correctly spaced, and facing the right direction! And when your child can form words correctly, he or she will be a better all-around student. Writing legibly and comfortably helps your child communicate with ease to allow time for thinking. Use the questions below to determine if your child needs help forming letters and words. If you answer yes to one or more of the questions, ask your child to select activities described in this section and complete them together. They're the "write" stuff!

DOES YOUR CHILD

- seem uncomfortable or unwilling to write?

- form letters, numbers, and words incorrectly, even when guided?

- frequently reverse letters and numbers?

- hold pencils and other writing instruments awkwardly or incorrectly?

- place writing paper in an awkward position on the table?

- incorrectly space paragraphs, letters within words, and words within sentences?

- switch from the left to right hand when writing?

- write letters "out of the lines"?

- have difficulty writing letters from memory?

The Alphabet in Print

Refer to this alphabet (or one provided by your child's teacher) for printing activities.

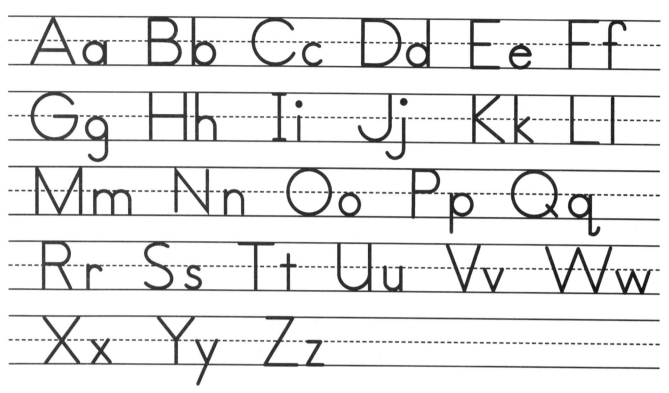

Aa Bb Cc Dd Ee Ff
Gg Hh Ii Jj Kk Ll
Mm Nn Oo Pp Qq
Rr Ss Tt Uu Vv Ww
Xx Yy Zz

The Alphabet in Cursive

Ask the teacher when cursive is taught in your child's school. If your child is learning cursive, refer to this alphabet (or one provided by your child's teacher) for cursive-writing activities.

Aa Bb Cc Dd Ee Ff
Gg Hh Ii Jj Kk Ll
Mm Nn Oo Pp Qq
Rr Ss Tt Uu Vv
Ww Xx Yy Zz

Family Time Reading Fun © 1997 Creative Teaching Press

In Perfect Form

(Using a Consistent Writing Style)

MATERIALS

print or cursive alphabet (page 72)

Help your child get into "perfect writing form" by having him or her make a quick phone call or write a note! Alphabet styles vary from teacher to teacher and school to school. Call or write your child's teacher and ask which form of writing is used and in which grade cursive is taught. Ask your child's teacher to send home either the print or cursive alphabet so you can use it at home. If your child's teacher does not have a preference, use an alphabet on page 72 as a guide and send a copy to the teacher. By using the same alphabet at home and school, you prevent confusion and frustration as your child learns to write.

Charted Waters

(Forming Words and Letters Correctly)

MATERIALS

print or cursive alphabet (page 72)
blank scrap paper
markers
tape

Chart letters so your child can sail into better writing! It's easy; just choose one alphabet with which to work—print or cursive. Write each upper- and lowercase letter pair on a piece of blank scrap paper to make several charts. Tape each chart on the wall where your child can see it when writing. Use the charts to remind your child how to form the letters. In addition, write on the chart any word that your child reverses (such as *tab* for *bat*) or cannot remember, highlighting the beginning letter. (Highlighting the beginning letter with a special color reminds your child where to start.) For example, if your child has difficulty remembering how to write his or her name, write his or her name on a chart with the first letter in a bright color. Remind your child to look at the charts while writing. Add to the charts from time to time. Take down charts as your child learns to write the displayed letters and words correctly.

Green Means Go

(Writing from Left to Right)

MATERIALS

green marker
writing paper

An important part of forming letters, words, and sentences is learning the direction in which to write. And there will be no stopping your child from writing words from left to right when you use *Green Means Go!* When your child is just beginning to write alone, draw a green dot at the left margin of each line on the paper. Explain that the dots represent the word *go* or *start.* Tell your child to go from the dot (the left margin) toward the right side of the paper when writing. Show your child where to start after he or she reaches the end of the line (to the green dot on the second line). Check understanding by asking questions such as *Where are you going to start? In what direction will you go? Where do you go when you finish writing on this line?* With a little practice, your child will go, go, go without the green!

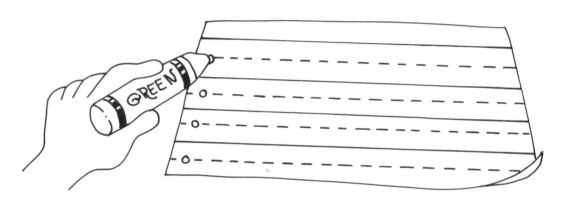

The Right Fit

(Finding the Right Writing Tools)

MATERIALS

different-size pencils
pencil grips
markers
unlined paper
ruler

Does your child have trouble forming letters and words? Sometimes the solution is as simple as changing writing tools! Experiment with different-size pencils, or buy some rubber or plastic grips that help smaller fingers hold thin pencils. Have your child try large markers to use in drawing; they are gripped easily and offer a smooth flow onto paper. If your child is a beginning writer, use unlined paper. It lessens frustration. If you feel your child needs lines, use a ruler to draw "bottom lines" across unlined paper. Try different writing tools until your child finds just the right fit!

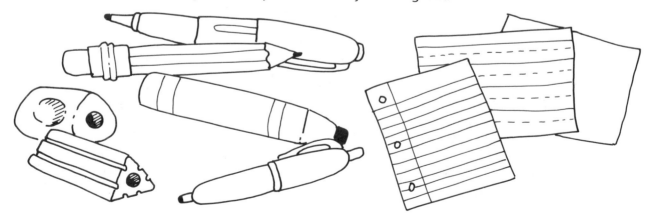

The Bottom Line

(Using the "Bottom Line" as a Guide When Writing)

MATERIALS

lined paper
unlined paper
ruler
pencil
print alphabet
(page 72)

After your child can write comfortably on unlined paper (see above), help him or her by "getting to the bottom of it." Here's how: After watching a favorite television show, invite your child to name four or five words that describe the show. Use the alphabet from your child's school or page 72 as a guide to write each word on lined paper as an "answer key." On unlined paper, draw a horizontal "bottom line" with a ruler for each word on the list. Encourage your child to look at the answer key and write each word on a line. For the first one or two words, carefully watch your child write and note if letters rest on the lines as seen on the letter charts. Help your child with the rest of the words. Write the dates on the list and save it in a folder as a record of your child's progress.

No Boundaries

(Exploring Letters and Words)

MATERIALS

print alphabet (page 72,
3-D sponge or foam letters,
alphabet chart, or alphabet
book)
unlined paper
pencil
file folder

If your child is a new writer, provide some practice with this fun activity! Invite your child to draw a picture on unlined paper. Discuss words that describe the picture. Invite your child to explore writing the words on a second piece of unlined paper, without worrying about spelling them correctly. Have your child either write spontaneously or look at a print alphabet for help with the letters. For the first one or two words, carefully watch your child write and note pencil grip, writing direction for each letter, and letter spacing. Help your child correctly form the letters and words as needed. Use this activity now and then for writing practice. Write the date on each drawing. Briefly write what you saw your child do as you watched. Save the samples and notes in a file folder as a record of how your child is growing as a writer.

Rainbow Word Trace-Over

(Exploring Letter Formation)

MATERIALS

poem or nursery rhyme
lined paper
print or cursive alphabet
(page 72)
writing samples
felt-tip markers
file folder

Invite your child to choose a few lines from a favorite poem or nursery rhyme. Copy the selection on lined paper, writing each word in a different color to show one word from another. Encourage your child to trace over each word in another single-color to form "rainbow word." Write the date on the writing sample. Use the activity from time to time, and keep the dated samples in a file folder to watch your child's writing grow over time!

At Close Range

(Forming Letters and Words)

MATERIALS

writing samples
lined paper
print or
cursive alphabet
(page 72)
file folder

As your child becomes confident tracing over letters and words (see above), have him or her copy words from the same paper first and then copy them on a different paper. For the "same paper" activity, copy a writing sample on every other line of a piece of lined paper. (Writing samples could include "to do" lists, notes, poems, lists, recipes, or food labels.) Have your child copy each word directly below the original. For the "different paper" activity, have your child copy your writing sample onto blank lined paper. For each activity, encourage your child to form the letters and words the way you have.

Write dates on each writing sample, and keep them in a file folder as a progress record. When your child can successfully copy at close range, have him or her practice distant copying (page 77).

Far, Far Away

(Copying Letters and Words From a Distance)

MATERIALS

print or cursive alphabet
(page 72)

telephone message

posterboard, wipe-off message
board, chalkboard, a large sheet
of paper, or paper-covered
cork board

markers or chalk

Copy a telephone message onto posterboard, a wipe-off message boar[d] a large sheet of paper, or paper-covered cork board. Place the mess[age] across from where your child sits to write. Have your child copy the writing sample onto paper similar to that used in school. Encourage your child to copy the letters and words just as they are formed. Use the copied message by giving it to the family member who received the call. Have your child practice distant copying from time to time so he or she experiences writing words and sentences for real-world purposes. Good handwriting isn't just for school!

Trace-Over Art

(Concentrating on How Letters Feel)

MATERIALS

construction paper or
newspaper

glue

yarn

scissors

print or cursive alphabet
(page 72)

This "artsy" activity can be used with Trace-Over (page 76) to increase your child's confidence and skill in forming letters and words. Neatly write your child's name on a large piece of construction paper or newspaper. Ask your child to carefully trace over the letters with glue and lay yarn over the glue. When dry, display the trace-over art for all to see. For more practice, repeat the activity with other favorite words such as names of family members or pets.

Sloppy Copy
(Gaining Confidence Forming Letters)

MATERIALS
writing paper

When your child has the freedom to make a "sloppy copy" before writing a second "good copy," he or she can concentrate on ideas first. To do this, have your child plan to make two copies when writing a short thank-you note, story, or report. Explain that the first copy (sloppy copy) is to practice getting ideas on paper. Do not stop your child to make instant corrections. Watch for signals that your child needs help, such as the frequent erasing of letters or words, spelling questions, or long pauses between writing. Encourage your child with a reminder that the sloppy copy is for practice. Read aloud and discuss the sloppy copy. Edit it with your child, and write the edited version under the first. Be sure to form your letters neatly and in the style your child is learning in school. Invite your child to copy the new version on a different piece of paper to make a "good copy." This time, help your child with forming letters and words. By using Sloppy Copy, your child will get helpful writing practice.

Finger Walk
(Spacing Paragraphs, Letters, and Words)

MATERIALS
writing paper

Learning spacing between paragraphs, letters within words, and words within sentences is at your child's fingertips! When beginning a paragraph, ask your child to place two fingers (from the free hand) along the left margin and across the top writing line. Have your child begin writing the first word of the paragraph on the right side of the two fingers (two spaces in). To explain letter-spacing within words, explain that he or she should not be able to slide a "pinkie" or "little finger" between the letters in a word. Model by writing a word with spread-out letters. Slide your pinkie between the letters to demonstrate. Write the word again more accurately, and show that you cannot slide a pinkie between the letters. To help him or her learn spacing between words, invite your child to place one finger (from the free hand) at the end of the word. Have your child begin writing the new word to the right side of his or her finger (leaving a space between words). Have your child use fingers to create space until it can be done without them.

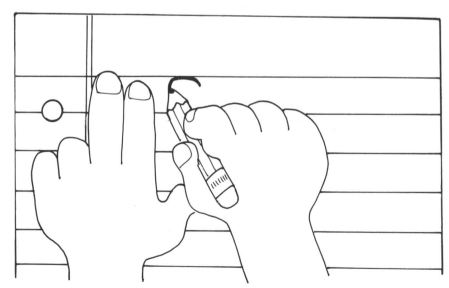

Feeling Good!

(Feeling How Letters, Numbers, and Words Are Formed)

MATERIALS

sand, table salt, or granulated sugar

cake or pie pan

index cards

markers

Sprinkle sand, table salt, or granulated sugar in an empty cake or pie pan so the bottom of the pan cannot be seen. Ask your child to choose several letters, numbers, or words to practice writing. Write each letter on an index card as your child names it. Place a card next to the pan in front of your child. First, have your child trace over the letter, number, or word on the card with a finger. Then have your child use this finger again and draw the same letter, number, or word in the pan, making an impression. Encourage your child to say the letter name, number, or word while drawing. Continue with all the cards. Play again whenever your child "feels" like it!

Call It Like You See It

(Recognizing Writing Stroke Names)

MATERIALS

writing paper

Call it like you see it and your child will learn to write it! Whenever your child works on forming letters and words, choose words to describe the strokes you want him or her to use. Talk with your child's teacher to find out the words he or she uses when teaching penmanship. Make a "writing word" list for yourself, and use it when helping your child form letters. For example, if your child writes the letter *m*, explain that you want him or her to make two *humps*. Repeat the word *hump* when describing how to write the letters *n* and *h*. Consistently say *undercurve* if you want your child to curve from the bottom of a letter up (as at the end of all cursive letters when they join another letter). Call circular movements *loops* or *ovals*. Whatever vocabulary you use, be consistent as your child grows as a writer.

A Smooth Transition

(Connecting Printing and Cursive Writing)

MATERIALS

writing paper

When it's time for the big switch to cursive, help your child make a smooth transition by modeling proper writing every day and doing the following activities together.

- Have your child print shopping or "to do" lists. Write each word in cursive next to the original. Compare the styles.

- Make two alphabet card sets, one in print, one in cursive. Have your child play Beat the Clock (page 31) and match the cards.

- Write all notes to your child and the teacher in cursive. Help your child read them.

Use your imagination and develop your own ways to show the connection; you can help your child see a clear purpose for writing in cursive.

Turn It Around

(Correctly Forming Letters, Numbers, and Words)

MATERIALS

writing paper
construction or
drawing paper
tape

Never fear, reversing letters, numbers, and words is a normal part of learning to write! Although any letter or number can be reversed, common letter and number reversals include *d* and *b, p* and *q, 3* and *5,* and *6* and *9.* Reversals can be words written from right to left or flip-flopping letters within a word. Keep a list of reversals your child makes when writing. Write the letters as part of words (such as *cab*) on construction or drawing paper to make a chart. Post the chart near your child's writing area. Invite your child to look at how words are formed on the chart when writing grocery lists, telephone messages, wish lists or any other set of words. (If your child consistently reverses letters or words, talk with the teacher. Ask whether the reversals are common for children of your child's age and experience. Your child's teacher will be able to offer extra help.) Use Rainbow Word Trace-Over and At Close Range (page 76) as other ways to help your child with reversals.

The Writing Process

Writing is a wonderful way for your child to share ideas, feelings, and a special part of himself or herself with others. To become a writer who can share all these things, your child needs to understand that writing is a process. The process of writing involves thinking about and organizing ideas, expressing ideas in meaningful words, and placing the words on paper. Use the questions below to determine if your child needs help with the writing process. If you answer yes to one or more of the questions, help your child select activities from this section and complete them together. Write away!

DOES YOUR CHILD

- have difficulty viewing himself or herself as a writer?

- have limited writing experiences (for few purposes and audiences)?

- fear criticism about his or her writing?

- seem uncomfortable and unwilling to write?

- view writing as a onetime event rather than a process?

- have difficulty transferring ideas to paper?

- fail to see the connection between reading, speaking, listening, and writing?

- fail to see the connection between writing and communicating real-life experiences?

- choose to consistently communicate through speaking rather than writing?

The Writing Process
(Seeing Writing as a Journey)

MATERIALS

writing paper

construction paper
(optional)

crayons, markers
(optional)

computer
(optional)

Does your child have a school assignment that will be displayed and should be "just right"? Use the writing process to help him or her complete the assignment and grow as a writer in the process! (Just a note: Not *all* writing should follow the writing process. For example, your child does not need to follow the process when writing lists, short notes, stories just for fun, or journal entries.) Discuss each step before writing begins. Use several pieces of paper to complete the steps so writing is not crowded or messy. The pride your child feels about his or her final product will keep him or her writing! Use the Writer's Guide (page 83) to guide your child during the writing process.

The Process

1   Have your child think about ideas he or she wants to share. Write a list of ideas about the subject or story or use an organizer (pages 56 to 58) to list ideas.

2   Help your child think about the ideas in order (from beginning to end) by asking questions about content.

3   Guide your child to write a first draft. Invite your child to ask questions when he or she needs help.

4   Discuss the first draft with your child. Point out strong points that make ideas clear and understandable for people who are reading the writing.

5   Edit and revise the first draft with your child to clear up ideas and correct spelling, grammar, and punctuation. (If you have a computer, use its word-processing "tools" such as spell-check, but teach your child to always proofread writing after it is printed. Computer programs do not edit ideas or catch all spelling and grammar mistakes!)

6   Have your child write a final draft in his or her best handwriting. If you have a computer and the teacher allows it, have your child write the draft on the computer.

7   Have your child write a title page, design a cover, draw an illustration, or generate a computer graphic.

"Write On"

(Gaining Purpose and a Clear Plan for Writing)

MATERIALS
Writer's Guide
(below)
writing paper

Your child's writing assignment will be "write on" the money when he or she answers writer's guide questions! As you and your child follow the writing process, ask the questions below. Encourage your child to think of answers before moving from step to step in the writing process.

Writer's Guide

1 Ideas

- Why are you writing this?
- Who will read what you write?
- Do you plan to display or publish your writing?
- What expectations does your teacher have?
- Have you been given guidelines or a rubric (grading sheet) that tells you what to do?
- What do you need to know to write what is expected?
- When will writing begin, and when do you have to be finished?

2 Ideas in Order

- Do you have a clear writing plan?
- What will you use to organize, save, and keep track of your writing?

3 First Draft

- Are your ideas understandable?
- Do your ideas flow naturally and make sense together?

4 Discuss

- Does your teacher want to see the first draft?
- Did you think about why you were writing and who you were writing for?
- Have you read your writing to make sure it is clear and meaningful?

5 Edit and Revise

- Have you carefully checked spelling and punctuation?
- What can you do to make your writing clear, fluent, and meaningful, with correct grammar?

6 Final Draft

- Have you made all the changes?
- Have you used your best handwriting?

7 Presentation

- How can you "show off" your final draft in an attractive, interesting way? with a picture? an interesting cover? a poster? a model?

Write Yourself

(Observing Writing in and out of School)

MATERIALS
writing paper

...he old saying *What you see is what you get* holds true when it concerns your child's desire to write. When your child sees you writing, he or she is more likely to choose to write. Whenever you can, have your child watch you write lists, checks, notes to friends, business letters, or even stories to share. From time to time, read your writing aloud and ask for your child's opinion. If your child offers good suggestions, make the changes. If you find mistakes as you read aloud, make changes as well; making changes shows your child that everyone has to revise his or her writing sometimes. So let your child see you write today, "write" away!

A Special Place

(Feeling Comfortable and Concentrating When Writing)

MATERIALS
table or desk
comfortable chair
good lighting
writing materials

Take a walk through the house with your child to choose a special place just for writing. If you can, set up a writing space in a quiet corner or out-of-the-way room. To make the chosen place really special, add a table or desk, a comfortable chair, good lighting, and writing materials such as pens, pencils, markers, crayons, and a variety of paper. Encourage your child to work in this special place whenever writing.

Personal Speller

(Improving Spelling When Writing)

MATERIALS

stapler

blank paper

markders, pens, pencils

A "personal speller" will help your child remember how to spell new words when writing. Staple blank sheets of paper together to make a 26-page booklet. Help your child write a letter of the alphabet (in order) at the top of each page. When writing a letter or story, invite your child to ask for help spelling a few key words that he or she needs. Ask your child to open the "personal speller" to the page with the first letter of each word. Write each word on its corresponding page, and have your child refer to the words throughout the writing session. Encourage your child to grow as a writer by using the "personal speller" whenver he or she writes.

Five Sense Fun

(Connecting the Five Senses with Writing)

MATERIALS

food new to your child

five senses chart (page 86)

writing paper

Put on your chef's hat and surprise your child with a new food and a new writing experience! Make a food new to your child. Use the five senses chart as a guide, and discuss the food. Ask your child to describe how the food looks, sounds (if sizzling or if it can be shaken), smells, feels, and tastes. Record your child's answers on the chart. Explain that it is sometimes easier to write something when a person talks about it first. Help your child write a few sentences to describe the food using words and ideas from the chart. Invite your child to read the sentences to the rest of the family, and have them guess the name of the food. Use the five senses chart from time to time when you want your child to focus on a subject for writing; it just makes sense!

Five Senses Chart

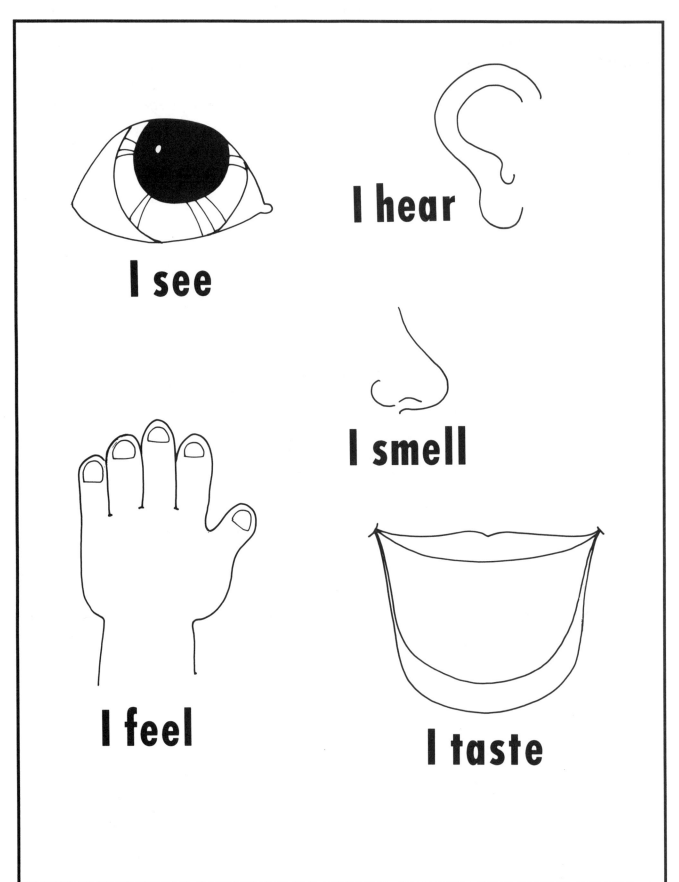

I see

I hear

I smell

I feel

I taste

Gifts for Writing

(Seeing Writing as an Important, Fun Activity)

MATERIALS

gifts associated with writing

Give the gift that lasts a lifetime . . . the gift of writing! Encourage your child to write by giving him or her gifts such as a variety of pens and pencils, a desk lamp, pads of paper, stationery, envelopes, stamps, a notebook for a diary or daily journal, a dictionary for your child's developmental level, or (if your child is older) a thesaurus. Give at least one "writing gift" every holiday or birthday. After giving the gift, show your child how to use it. Your time together will be fun and well spent!

Be on the Lookout

(Gaining Writing Skills by Writing Frequently)

MATERIALS

writing paper

Be on the lookout for opportunities for your child to write! Offer opportunities every day. Writing could include diary entries, grocery lists, holiday and birthday cards, telephone messages, notes to friends, trip planning, thank-you notes, or even party invitations. No writing task is too small; each gives excellent practice! (Be patient if your child seems hesitant to write. There may be times when writing interest is high and others when it is low.) Keep watching, keep offering, and keep encouraging; soon your child will be naturally writing to you!

Create a Caption

(Focusing on and Completing a Writing Task)

MATERIALS

photographs
scrapbook or photo album
writing paper
scissors
tape or photo adhesive
page decorations (stickers,
rubber stamps,
paper cutouts)

Remember special times by giving your child a little writing practice with this fun activity! Invite your child to create a scrapbook or photo album for a special family event. Attach photos from the event in a scrapbook or photo album. Ask your child to write photo captions on paper, cut them out to fit on the pages, and attach them with tape or photo adhesive. For extra fun, have your child make and attach dialogue-filled "speech bubbles" to the photos. Invite your child to finish the pages with stickers, rubber stamps, or paper cutouts. Display the scrapbook or photo album on a table, and invite your child to share it with friends and family.

Write Away

(Writing for a Variety of Purposes)

MATERIALS

magazines, cereal
boxes, newspapers
envelopes
stamps

Get out the stamps; after your child writes a letter and receives something in return, he or she won't want to stop! Encourage your child to read magazines, cereal boxes, and newspapers to find addresses for information packets, free samples, travel brochures, contests, giveaways, or anything free of charge. Show your child how to write letters that ask for items and information. Help address envelopes and send the letters. Writing will have so much more meaning when your child sees real results from his or her hard work!

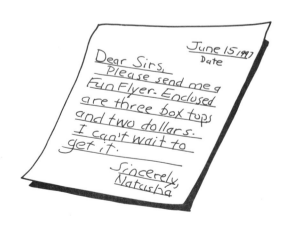

Notice the "Good Stuff"

(Becoming a Willing, Confident Writer)

MATERIALS

This one's easy. All you have to do is notice the "good stuff"! Whenever you can, acknowledge your child's writing accomplishments. Focus on content, spelling, punctuation, and mechanical accomplishments. Emphasize your child's writing successes by using phrases such as

- *Your writing is well organized.*

- *The first sentence in this paragraph is very clear and understandable.*

- *Your ideas for the story are well-thought out.*

- *I like how you described the setting. It makes me feel as though I'm there.*

- *The events in your summary are in order. Good job!*

- *Your story made me laugh.*

- *I can see you are checking your spelling and proofreading more carefully.*

When you notice the "good stuff," it will keep happening!

Perfect Pen Pals

(Writing for a Purpose)

MATERIALS

notes, letters, and e-mail
from relatives and friends
writing paper or computer
letter guide (page 90)
envelopes
stamps

Make a call to relatives and friends and ask them to write notes and letters and send e-mail to your child. Have your child write back. Copy the letter guide (page 90) to help your child fill in the blanks to write a letter in the correct form. Help address envelopes and send the letters. The form will no longer be needed when your child can remember the parts of a letter. But keep the letter-writing going; your child will become a better writer and could have pen pals for years to come!

Letter Guide

_____
Date

Dear_____ ,

_____

_____

_____

_____

_____

_____

_____

_____

_____

_____

_____

_____

_____

_____ ,

_____

Organization & Study Skills

● ●

When your child has good organization and study skills, his or her mind is more "open" for learning! Being prepared and knowing how to learn helps your child concentrate on the important tasks of thinking, listening, speaking, reading, and writing. Use the questions below to determine if your child needs help with organization and study skills. If you answer yes to one or more of the questions, help your child select activities from this section and complete them together. Your child will have tools to become more orderly, organized, and "open" to learning!

DOES YOUR CHILD

● have difficulty making decisions or establishing priorities for completing a task?

● forget assignments or lose papers, crayons, books, and other supplies?

● have difficulty following directions?

● have difficulty completing assignments?

● fail to see the connection between learning and future plans?

● struggle with managing time?

● have difficulty taking responsibility for work?

● depend on others for completing a task?

● blame others when work is incorrect or incomplete?

Real-World Reading

(Connecting the Real World and Learning at School)

MATERIALS

Why Read? sheet (page 93)

Help your child answer the question *Why is it important to learn to read?* by completing the following thought-provoking activity. Discuss careers and have your child name three favorites. Ask your child to think about those careers and complete Why Read? on page 93 together. After completing each section, discuss it. When the whole page is complete, ask your child *Why is it important to learn to read?*; you should get a real-world answer!

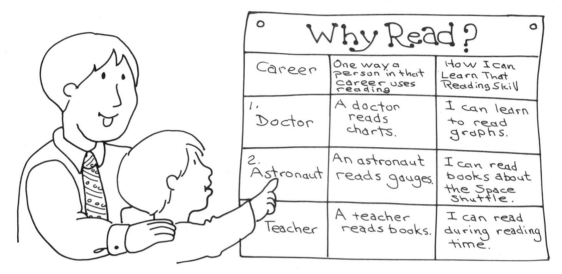

Why Read?		
Career	One way a person in that career uses reading	How I can Learn That Reading Skill
1. Doctor	A doctor reads charts.	I can learn to read graphs.
2. Astronaut	An astronaut reads gauges.	I can read books about the Space Shuttle.
Teacher	A teacher reads books.	I can read during reading time.

Parent/Student/Teacher Meeting

(Setting Clear, Appropriate Expectations)

MATERIALS

writing paper

If your child seems continually frustrated with schoolwork, or unable to read or write as expected, have a parent/student/teacher meeting to set some realistic goals. First, make a list of progress-related questions and concerns with your child. Bring the list to share at the meeting. Discuss what learning you see at home, and ask about expectations at school. Together, look at some daily work that shows your child's progress. Share samples of reading and writing experiences from home. Work with the teacher and your child to create a clear set of realistic expectations for home and school. Write them down for everyone to see. Read the expectations with your child from time to time. It's a great reminder, and a huge "ego booster" when your child sees progress!

Why Read?

Career	One Way a Person in That Career Uses Reading	How I Can Learn That Reading Skill
1.		
2.		
3.		

Demonstration Station

(Completing Each Step of an Assignment)

MATERIALS

items for completing a short task (such as preparing a recipe, fixing a flat tire, gardening vegetables, etc.) writing paper

Choose an interesting household job such as preparing a recipe, fixing a flat tire, or gardening vegetables. Invite your child to watch and help while you complete it. Talk while you work; explain each step, and discuss what you want to accomplish. After your demonstration, review the steps with your child, and ask your child what you did to achieve your goal. Explain that an important part of organization for school is completing each step of an assignment, just as you did in the real-life job. Invite your child to join you in completing tasks that lead to a goal. Occasionally, demonstrate for your child what needs to be done to achieve goals for school assignments.

Take Charge

(Setting Goals)

MATERIALS

activity planner (page 95) file folder

Have your child choose an academic goal such as learning addition tables, writing his or her last name legibly, or learning five facts about your state. Write the goal and display it on the activity planner. Invite your child to plan activities to help achieve the goal. Offer activity suggestions, but have your child take the responsibility for deciding the final plans. Write the activity ideas on the activity planner for your child. Help your child complete the activities and then offer congratulations. Discuss the activities by asking questions such as *How did you feel when you got to choose an activity? Did the activity work? Why or why not? What did you learn? What would you do differently next time? What would you do the same? Did you meet your goal? Why or why not?* Complete the rest of the planner and identify what your child describes as evidence that the goal was met. Record the date completed. Store activity planners in a file folder to show growth over time.

Activity Planner

Goal: I will _____

Three Activity Ideas to Achieve My Goal:

1. _____

   _____

2. _____

   _____

3. _____

   _____

	Date Begun	What I Did	Date Completed	Evidence that I Achieved My Goal
Activity One				
Activity Two				
Activity Three				

Break It Up

(Setting Goals and Completing Complex Assignments)

MATERIALS

school assignment
writing paper

Breaking up is easy to do with this sensible activity! Help your child manage a complex school assignment by breaking it up into smaller steps. Before beginning the assignment, discuss the steps necessary to complete it. Ask questions such as *How will you know when you are finished? What do you have to do to get to the "finish line"?* Have your child name each step necessary to finish the assignment. List each step on paper. Help your child set a time limit for each step's completion. Invite your child to refer to the steps (and modify them if necessary) while completing the assignment. Congratulate your child each time a step is completed.

My Study Schedule

(Taking Responsibility for Completing Assignments)

MATERIALS

clock or timer
school
assignments

It's not how long you study, it's how well. Help your child concentrate on or finish assignments by setting an easy-to-follow study schedule. Ask your child to select 15- or 30-minute study sessions throughout the day. For example, your child may choose to study for 15 minutes as soon as he or she gets home from school, just before and immediately after supper, or just before bedtime. With a study schedule planned specifically by your child, the question becomes *When did you say you needed to study?* rather than *When did I tell you …?*

Tell Me More

(Gaining a Sense of Accomplishment)

MATERIALS

Don't just tell your child that you like something he or she has done, tell why! Sincerely acknowledge an accomplishment when your child completes a task. Avoid generalities such as *Good job.* Instead, be specific and say something like *Thank you for taking the trash out without being reminded. How does it feel when I don't have to remind you?; I see that you looked at the clock and began working at 4:30. How does it feel to be finished before dinner?; You put all your toys away. Does that make you as happy as it makes me?;* or *The dog looks terrific. Thank you for brushing her!* Feeling a sense of accomplishment upon completing a task at home will encourage your child to complete tasks in school as well.

To Do Lists

(Remembering Commitments)

MATERIALS

notebook, calendar, or formal assignment book

"To do" lists aren't just for grown-ups; your child can benefit from them, too. Help your child pick out a special "list keeper," such as a notebook, calendar, or formal assignment book. Together, list specific "to do" goals each week, such as visit special places, shop for weekly lunch food, or complete assignments. (If your child is very young or does not feel confident writing words, invite him or her to draw pictures.) At the end of each day, spend a few minutes reviewing goals that were met and check them off. Move goals not accomplished to another day. Update the list each week and then congratulate your child for all those check marks!

Down to a System
(Getting Organized)

MATERIALS

small storage containers (cardboard and plastic boxes, files, notebooks with dividers, pocket folders)

labels

backpack

Do you hear *Have you seen my homework?* or *Where is my backpack?* more than once a month? Try this! Have your child gather several small storage containers for crayons, pencils, papers, and other supplies. Set a time to meet and help your child clean out his or her desk or cubbie. Have your child place loose items in a container. Show your child how to stack textbooks from smallest to largest. Go through your child's backpack. Help organize it and designate pockets for lunch money, notes home, and homework. From time to time, help your child take inventory and put things back in order. Your child will soon understand that a little time beforehand will save a lot of time later!

Ask More and Tell Less
(Taking Responsibility)

MATERIALS

Ask questions rather than giving assignments to help your child "get it done" and develop a sense of responsibility. Instead of saying *You are supposed to meet the bus at 8:00,* ask *What time are you supposed to meet the bus?* Other questions might include *What homework do you have today? How long do you think it will take? What time will you start?* or *When will you clean your room today?* Your child will quickly and confidently complete tasks at home and at school when feeling self-motivated and responsive; now that's "getting it done"!

Attitudes & Interests

A positive attitude and a high interest level for learning can make your child's future bright! When your child cares about and wants to learn new things, he or she is more apt to learn, and learn quickly. Use the folllowing questions to determine if your child needs help gaining a greater interest in or a positive attitude toward learning. If you answer yes to one or more of the questions, help your child select activities from this section and complete them together. The activities are fun and will help your child become interested in learning.

DOES YOUR CHILD

- have a negative or "I don't care" attitude about listening, speaking, reading, or writing?

- seem to lack purpose when expected to use literacy skills?

- show signs of frustration when attempting to think, listen, speak, read, or write?

- fail to view himself or herself as a thinker, listener, speaker, reader, and writer?

- consistently say *I don't know* when asked questions?

- arrive late to school almost every day?

Reading All Around

(Developing an Interest in Reading)

MATERIALS

real-world reading materials (magazine and newspaper articles, stories, recipes, advertisements, letters)

Fun opportunities for reading and learning are everywhere; and all you have to do is show your child where to look! It's easy; whenever you get the chance, read aloud. Casually read aloud and discuss magazine and newspaper articles, stories, recipes while cooking, advertisements, and letters. By these simple actions, you are showing that reading is all around and you are developing your child's interest in learning, creating a positive attitude, and laying groundwork for understanding what eventually will be read without you.

Shout It Loud, I'm So Proud!

(Viewing Oneself as a Learner)

MATERIALS

Help your child gain a positive attitude about learning by showing your sincere pride in him or her. Acknowledge your child's efforts and achievements. Display work on a refrigerator, window, or bathroom mirror; or save it in a special notebook or scrapbook. Support good effort outside of school in areas such as sports, music, or citizenship. (Confidence outside of school can transfer to greater confidence in school.) Show your pride by smiling, patting your child on the back, giving the "thumbs up," or sharing a proud word. These are rewards money cannot buy. Be sincere. Do not overdo praise or let it become an automatic, empty reaction your child will tune out. Do what you can to shout it loud, and tell your child *I'm so proud!*

Make a Game of It

(Creating a Positive Attitude about Learning)

MATERIALS
egg or oven timer
writing paper

Make studying for a test into a game and turn potential failure into sure success. Have your child study a small portion of the material to be tested, and then play a game. Give an answer to one of the test questions and have your child think of a question to match the answer. Repeat with four more answers. Have your child study some more and give five more questions. Continue with answers and questions until all the material is reviewed. Explain that work can be finished more accurately and quickly when we concentrate on one small part at a time.

Wonderful Words

(Lessening Frustration for Learning)

MATERIALS
none

When discussing schoolwork or any of your child's efforts, use some "wonderful words" to get your ideas across. Be sure to speak honestly and respectfully. Even when your child's efforts do not meet your expectations, show your feelings in a kind, respectful manner. Do not assume your child knows that you appreciate his or her efforts, however successful. Describe specifically what you notice to show you care. When you use sincere words, wonderful things can start to happen for your child.

Good-Work Meeting Day
(Creating a Positive Self-Image)

MATERIALS

container for schoolwork

schoolwork samples

Have a good-work meeting day and watch your child's self-esteem and learning grow! Use a special container for your child's schoolwork, such as a wicker basket, old tool box, or an over-size tennis shoe. Have your child place the work in the container each day. Designate a special day each week as "good-work meeting day." Before meeting with your child, go through the schoolwork and choose two or three samples that show good work and one for setting a future goal. Invite your child to do the same. (Do not remove the samples from the container. You and your child may choose the same examples.) During the meeting, invite your child to share the chosen samples and tell why they show good work and why a future goal is needed. Share your samples and explain why you chose them. Have your child clean out the container after each meeting so it is ready for all new work. Your emphasis on good work will reinforce effort, nurture pride, and can keep your child growing as a learner.

Make Meaning
(Gaining a Sense of Purpose for Learning)

MATERIALS

poems or tongue twisters

Offer meaningful reading and writing experiences so your child will develop a purpose for learning. Avoid exercises that expect your child to recite or copy words or letters over and over in isolation without explaining the purposes for the repetitive actions. Instead, read to and encourage your child to memorize or write poems or tongue twisters that use the key words or letters so your child gets practice using them in a natural way.

The Home–School Connection

(Developing an "I Care" Attitude about Learning)

MATERIALS
telephone
writing paper
homemade gifts
(optional)

Make a positive connection with your child's school, and watch your child be m... too. When your child sees your respectful, positive attitude about the school, teacher, a... curriculum, he or she is more likely to develop a similar attitude. Call the principal and/or teacher when you observe a special program, project, or assignment that helped your child grow academically or personally. Write thank-you notes or send homemade gifts to people who help your child learn. Surprise your child at school by taking him or her out to lunch. Volunteer when you can—help during the day as a "room parent," tutor after school, or get involved in special events on weekends. Show your excitement about and support for academic, sporting, and social events; make the connection today!

Less May Be Best

(Lessening Frustration)

MATERIALS
notebook

Take the "less can be best" approach by taking a close look at your child's work habits during several short, medium, and long assignments. Assignments should be related to one skill such as learning spelling words or recalling story sequence. On dated entries in a notebook, write down how long your child took to complete the assignments (if they were completed), and take notes about his or her attitude and success (number correct, neatness, etc.). Meet with your child's teacher and share the entries. Discuss what you saw and together decide the assignment-length needed to produce the best results. For some children, a lot of work does more harm than good. If "less is best," make the changes at home and school; shorten assignments to help your child learn more and feel frustrated less!

Positive Role Models

(Gaining a Sense of Purpose for Learning)

MATERIALS

literature and videotapes about famous people

writing paper

Your child's favorite sports figures, movie stars, musicians, and singers can help him or her learn! Gather books, magazine and newspaper articles, and videos about two or three positive role models. With your child, read about each famous person. Discuss their struggles and triumphs. Help your child find addresses for the famous people. (Addresses are available through public relations offices, the World Wide Web, or magazines such as *Sports Illustrated for Kids* and *Bop*.) Have your child write and ask for pictures or written replies.

Time Capsule

(Gaining a Sense of Purpose for Learning)

MATERIALS

writing paper

paper towel tube

markers

You can motivate your child by having some fun with your child's favorite careers. Have your child choose a career such as firefighter, F.B.I. agent, scientist, gymnast, or veterinarian. Discuss the career, and explain how learning in school will help your child get that job. On a piece of writing paper, write the date and your child's career choice. Roll the paper and place it in a paper towel tube. Label the tube *Time Capsule*. Place the time capsule in a safe location. After three or four months, ask your child to name a career goal again. (It may or may not be the same.) Pull the paper from the time capsule and compare the choices. Discuss how some goals change and some stay the same. Discuss the new (or same) career choice, and explain how learning in school will help your child get that job. Write the date and second career choice on the paper, and put it back in the time capsule. From time to time, remove the time capsule and have your child add career goals to it. As you discuss the different careers listed, your child will begin to see how our goals may change over time but the importance of doing well in school remains the same.

Career Field Trip

(Becoming Interested in Learning)

MATERIALS

writing paper
envelopes (optional)
stamps
(optional)

Take a career field trip with your child today, and help him or her in school tomorrow! Ask your child to name a career goal. Arrange visits to workplaces and personal meetings with people in that profession (such as a graphic designer, firefighter, F.B.I. agent, or scientist). Prepare your child by helping him or her write a list of questions to ask. If you cannot arrange a face-to-face meeting, help your child write and send letters to find out how people in this career achieved their goals and what they did to prepare for their profession.

Class Act

(Making Learning Fun)

MATERIALS

current topic of study
props (household
items, clothing)

Help your child make learning fun by acting. Choose a concept or theme from a current topic of study, such as math story problems, historical events, stories from reading instruction, scientific discoveries, or specific writing lessons. Have your child act out the concept and share information about it with you and others. (He or she could also pretend to be the teacher giving a silly, but factual, lesson.) For example, your child could demonstrate multiplication by pretending to be a chef who doubles a recipe (with many mishaps and theatrics). Invite your child to make props from household items and clothing. Help him or her practice, and offer assistance when needed. Gather the family, and have your child perform a "class act"!

Role Reversal

(Viewing Oneself as a Learner)

MATERIALS
school-related questions

From time to time, invite your child to quiz you with school-related questions, such as spelling, math, or science questions, or questions about a story you just read together. Even if your child does not know the answers "without looking," he or she will gain confidence by becoming the expert, the one who asks the questions and has the answers at hand. Use role reversal from time to time; your child will be a teacher while learning!

Not-a-Bore Chore

(Becoming Actively Involved in Learning)

MATERIALS
childhood chore

Household chores are excellent learning opportunities! To turn a chore into a learning experience, try this activity. Choose a chore new to your child, such as weeding the garden, emptying the trash cans, or sorting the mail. Demonstrate the chore instead of telling your child how to do it. Then have your child do what you do. Discuss why the chore is important to your family. Your child will grow more positive and confident by making an important contribution to the family.

Important People

(Gaining a Sense of Purpose for Learning)

MATERIALS
literature and videotapes explaining the lives and views of influential people and decision makers
writing paper
envelopes
stamps

Sometime this year, explore together the views of "important people" (politicians, scientists, business people, celebrities, journalists—anyone who influences public opinion or affects public policy.) Discuss what these people believe in and "stand for," and have your child choose one with whom he or she strongly agrees or disagrees. Talk together and help your child form healthy, logical, well-thought out opinions regarding the person's issue. Have your child dictate a letter to the "important person" and ask questions, state an opinion, and ask for a reply. Write the letters in your child's words and send them. You will empower your child when you invite opinions about real issues; that feeling of strength will carry over at home and at school.

A Health Issue?

(Ruling Out Health Problems)

MATERIALS
health observation
(page 108)

If, despite every effort, your child remains discouraged or negative about learning, or cannot read and write after diligently trying, consider a complete physical examination, including vision and hearing testing. Ask yourself the questions on the health observation (page 108) and offer the information to the health care provider during a physical exam. The health observation is a *partial* list of questions; your pediatrician will have a complete list. (For an explanation of how physical characteristics can affect literacy development, see pages 12 to 14.) Never give up. Keep looking for a solution. Eventually, you and your child will find solutions together!

Health Observation

HEARING

Does Your Child

- have frequent ear infections or fluid buildup?
- have severe allergies?
- become frustrated with listening or following-directions activities?
- know a letter sound one moment and forget it the next?
- have difficulty discriminating between similar-sounding words?
- become restless or seem distracted when listening to a story?

VISION

Does Your Child

- have red or watery eyes?
- look as though his or her eyes are not working together?
- squint or cover an eye?
- say *I have a headache; My eyes itch; or I can't see things on the board?*
- lose his or her place when reading?
- write poorly or cannot stay on the lines?
- use a hand or fingers to keep his or her place when reading or writing?
- get tired easily when reading?
- read a little at a time and then look away frequently?

GENERAL HEALTH

Does Your Child

- wake up frequently or sleep at irregular intervals?
- drink a lot of caffeine?
- eat a lot of sugar or food with preservatives?
- have difficulty with gross- or fine-motor skills?
- have allergies?

Resources

● ● ● ● ● ● ● ● ● ● ● ●

Books

The following books are recommended for obtaining additional information on helping your child with literacy:

Baghban, Marcia, (1989) *You Can Help Your Young Child with Writing;* (1990) *Ayude a su niño con la escritura* (Spanish), International Reading Association.

Cairney, Trevor and Lynne Munsie, (1995) *Beyond Tokenism: Parents As Partners in Literacy,* Heinemann.

Clay, Marie, (1988) *Writing Begins at Home: Preparing Children for Writing before They Go to School,* Heinemann.

Cullinan, Bernice and Brod Bagert, (1993) *Helping Your Child Learn to Read,* A.F.T. and U.S. Department of Education.

Delgado-Gaitan, Concha, (1990) *Literacy for Empowerment: The Role of Parents in Children's Education,* Falmer Press.

Fredericks, Anthony D., (1993) *Involving Parents through Children's Literature, preschool–kindergarten;* (1992) *Involving Parents through Children's Literature, grades 1–2;* (1993) *Involving Parents through Children's Literature, grades 3–4;* (1993) *Involving Parents through Children's Literature, grades 5–6;* (1997) *The Librarian's Complete Guide to Involving Parents through Children's Literature,* Teacher Ideas Press.

Fredericks, Anthony D., (1987) *Parent Letters for Early Learning; Letters for Parents,* Scott Foresman and Co.

Gentry, J. Richard (1996) *Helping Your Kid Learn to Spell.* Heinemann.

Gentry, J. Richard, (1987) *Spel . . . Is a Four-Letter Word,* Heinemann.

Glazer, Susan Mandel, (1990) *Creating Readers and Writers,* International Reading Association.

Grinnell, Paula C., (1989) *How Can I Prepare My Young Child for Reading?,* International Reading Association (Parent Booklet).

Hannon, Peter, (1995) *Literacy, Home, and School: Research and Practice in Teaching Literacy with Parents,* Falmer Press.

Harris, Theodore L., and Richard E. Hodges, Editors (1995) *The Literacy Dictionary: The Vocabulary of Reading and Writing,* International Reading Association.

Hill, Mary W., (1989) *Home: Where Reading and Writing Begin,* Heinemann.

Itzkoff, Seymour W., (1996) *Children Learning to Read: A Guide for Parents and Teachers,* Praeger Publishing.

Leonhardt, Mary, (1993) *Parents Who Love Reading, Kids Who Don't: How It Happens and What You Can Do About It,* Random House.

Michel, Pamela A., (1994) *The Child's View of Reading: Understandings for Teachers and Parents*, Allyn and Bacon.

Roser, Nancy L., (1990) *Helping Your Child Become a Reader*, International Reading Association.

Silvern, Steven, and Linda R. Silvern, (1990) *Beginning Literacy and Your Child*, International Reading Association.

Smith, Carl B., (1991) *Help Your Child Read and Succeed: A Parent's Guide*, Grayson Bernard Publishers.

Stoll, Donald R., Editor, (1997) *Magazines for Kids and Teens*, International Reading Association.

Taylor, Denny, and Dorothy Strickland, (1983) *Family Storybook Reading*, Heinemann.

Topping, Keith J., (1995) *Paired Reading, Spelling, and Writing: The Handbook for Teachers and Parents*, Cassell.

Topping, Keith J. and Sheila Wolfendale, Editors, (1985) *Parental Involvement in Children's Reading*, Nichols Publishing.

Trelease, Jim, (1992) *Hey! Listen to This: Stories to Read Aloud;* (1995)*The Read-Aloud Handbook*, Penguin Books.

Weinberger, Jo, (1996) *Literacy Goes to School: The Parents' Role in Young Children's Literacy Learning*, Paul Chapman Publishing.

Yopp, Hallie Kay, (March, 1995) "Read-Aloud Books for Developing Phonemic Awareness: An Annotated Bibliography," *The Reading Teacher*, pages 538–542, International Reading Association.

Technology

The following are literacy resources that can be reached through the World Wide Web, e-mail, and/or mail or telephone.

American Library Association
(Information about award-winning children's books and parent resources)
Association for Library Service to Children (ALSC)
50 East Huron St., Chicago, IL 60611
Telephone: (312) 944-6780
Internet address: *http://www.ala.org/alsc/*

American Speech-Language-Hearing Association (ASHA)
(Advocate for people with communication disorders)
10801 Rockville Pike, Rockville , MD 20852
Telephone: (301) 897-5700
FAX: (301) 571-0457
e-mail: *webmaster@asha.org*
Internet address: *http://www.asha.org/abash.htm*

The Children's Book Council, Inc. (CBC)
(Information about children's literature and book publishing)
568 Broadway, Suite 404, New York, NY 10012
Telephone: (212) 966-1990
FAX: (212) 966-2073
e-mail: *staff@CBCBooks.org*
Internet address: *http://www.CBCBooks.org*

ERIC Clearinghouse on Disabilities and Gifted Education
(Information about the education and development of gifted and disabled persons)
The Council for Exceptional Children (EC)
1920 Association Drive, Reston, VA 20191
Telephone: 1-800-328-0272
e-mail: *ericec@cec.sped.org*
Internet address: *http://www.cec.sped.org/ericec.htm*

ERIC Clearinghouse on Elementary and Early Childhood Education
(Information about child development, teaching young children, parenting, and family life)
University of Illinois at Urbana-Champaign
Children's Research Center
51 Gerty Drive, Champaign, IL 61820-7469
Telephone: 1-800-583-4135
FAX: (217) 333-3767
e-mail: *ericeece@uiuc.edu*
Internet address: *http://ericps.uiuc.edu/eece*

ERIC Clearinghouse on Reading, English, and Communication
(Information about parent involvement in reading)
Indiana University
Smith Research Center
1805 E. 10th Street, Suite 150, Bloomington, IN 47408-2698
Phone: (812) 855-5847; Fax: (812) 855) 855-4220
Internet addresses: *http://www.indiana.edu/~eric_rec/*

International Reading Association
(Resources for educators; Special interest group on parent involvement)
800 Barksdale Road
P.O. Box 8139, Newark, DE 19711-8139
Telephone: 302-731-1600
FAX: 302-731-1057
e-mail: *74673.3646@compuserve.com*
Internet address: *http://www.reading.org/*

Library of Congress, Children's Literature Center
(Reference and bibliographic assistance for the use of over two hundred thousand children's books)
Thomas Jefferson, Room LJ-100, Washington, D.C. 20540-4620
e-mail: *lcweb@loc.gov*
Internet addresses: (Library of Congress)*http//lcweb.loc.gov/*
(Children's Literature Center)*http://lcweb.loc.gov/folklife/fr_child.html*

National Association for the Education of Young Children
(Information and support for early childhood education)
1509-16th St. N.W., Washington, DC 20036-1426
Telephone: 1-800-424-2460 (Toll-free)
FAX: (202) 328-1846
e-mail: *pubaff@naeyc.org*
Internet address: *http://www.america-tomorrow.com/naeyc/*

National Council of Teachers of English
(Information and ideas for English and language arts instruction)
Parent and community resources available on-line)
1111 Kenyon Rd., Urbana, IL 61801
Telephone: (217) 328-3870
Internet address: *http://www.ncte.org/parents/list.html*

National Information Center for Children and Youth with Disabilities
(Information on disability-related issues for families and educators of children and youth; Spanish available)
P.O. Box 1492, Washington, D.C. 20013-1492
e-mail: *nichcy@aed.org*
Internet address: *http://www.aed.org/nichcy/*

National Parents and Teachers Association Headquarters
(Largest volunteer association working on behalf of children and youth)
Office of Governmental Relations
Washington, D.C.
Telephone: (202) 289-6790
Internet address: *http://pta.org/pta/*

The Orton Dyslexia Socity
(Explores research and treatment of dyslexia)
International Office
8600 La Salle Rd., Chester Building, Suite 382, Baltimore, MD 21286-2044
Telephone: (800) ABCD-123
Internet address: *http://ods.org*

Read-Write-Now (RWN)
U. S. Department of Education
(Assists families in fostering good literacy habits; Assists schools and youth organizations in improving reading and writing abilities)
Internet address: *http://www.udel.edu/ETL/RWN/RWN.html*